Awesome Life

Create the life you always wanted and soar with purpose!

Ahsan Khan & Shazad Ahmad

Disclaimer

All ideas, opinions and concepts in this book are for information and education purposes only. The authors and the Publisher bear no liability in connection with the use of the ideas presented. The authors are not giving any form of medical advice. Please consult a competent professional whether medical or otherwise for detailed advice that is appropriate to your health and overall situation in life.

Care has been given to source and cite material in this book. If any error or omission has occurred, it is sincerely regretted by the authors and will be rectified in future editions.

ISBN 978-0-9947974-0-7 (for print)
ISBN 978-0-9947974-1-4 (for eBook)

Library of Congress Cataloguing in Publication Data
Khan, Ahsan & Ahmad, Shazad
Awesome Life

1. Foreword 2. Introduction 3. Goals make us awesome 4. Time investment 5. Magnetic personality 6. Character: be the guy 7. Amazing health 8. Equanimity 9. Kicking the worry habit 10. Meditation and mindfulness 11. Happy marriage 12. Public speaking 13. Pursuit of happiness 14. Lifelong learning 15. Epilogue

Cover Design: Rishi Israni
Cover Photo: Getty Images
Editors: Sara Jamil & Kathleen Conway

Printed in Canada
Jamnik Graphics, Vaughan, Ontario

Dedication

This book is dedicated to a person
who truly represents being **Awesome**.
In the brief time she was among us,
she earned the admiration of all who met her
and those who only heard about her.
She inspired people by her example and was so charming
that she can never be forgotten.

Her name is Tanya Khan.

Table of Contents

Foreword

Why we wrote this book

This is a book about personal development, a topic that both of us enjoy tremendously. If there is a good book out there on the subject, we probably read it and therefore we stand on the shoulders of giants. In that sense, we acknowledge that we are not writing anything new; however, we hope, compelling and inspiring, nonetheless. We have personally studied and followed these concepts and know they work. Life is exciting and enjoyable when you have purpose and direction. We want to share this message and its wisdom with people through this book. The process of writing this book has also been a self-reflection exercise for both of us and has helped to clarify our thinking and validate our belief that there is more to life than just accepting what life throws at you. We most definitely are treading the path of self-improvement and personal development and suspect we will be doing so till we take our last breaths.

We wrote this book in a style that is different from most books of this genre. If you enjoy reading such books, you will notice that the majority of them do not mention the link between one's own determination and the help of one's Creator as being instrumental. As such, we have written this book with deliberate reference to spirituality and have drawn inspiration from many respected luminaries of history, who were no doubt spiritual people, and also from scriptures of the world's great religions. Ultimately, we hope that all readers will find something in this book that is of personal benefit to them and that they will feel motivated to keep pursuing a life that is Awesome! If we ever get a pat on the back, that will be the icing on the cake for us.

We started talking about doing this project at least six

years ago and let the idea take flight and fade a few times before we got serious. In February of 2013, we finally set up a schedule to start writing and made a regular Monday night call to update each other. We have no idea how you will feel about our effort, but we sincerely hope you will like our book. Most of all, we hope you will always have an Awesome Life!

Acknowledgements

Finishing this book has filled our hearts with gratitude and amazement. We did it! The emphasis is on we. First and foremost, we thank God Almighty for being able to follow through and achieve this goal. Next, we thank our friends who have helped us bring this book to its completion. They provided us with valuable feedback and encouragement that we are on to something good. We are indebted to all of them: Waheed Ahmad, Gaye Fullerton, Mirza Muhammad Afzal, Patrick Bartlett, Aamer Zuberi, Kathleen Conway, Mahmood Shaikh, Tariq Tahir, Sohail Ahmad, Mukarram Nazeer, Emmanuel Bulaclac, Atif Mir, Naeem Bhatti, Zena Alrawdah, Mamoon Rashid, Sara Jamil, Lisette Logan, and our mothers! We thank you all for your valuable time and help.

Ahsan & Shazad
August 2015

Introduction

We all get one life to live. However, in the short span of this life, we spend the first twenty years just preparing for it. In the years after that, the University of Life or the School of Hard Knocks, gives us the lessons necessary to live our best lives. Often, we learn a lesson and wish we knew it earlier in life. If we had learned that lesson sooner, we would now be farther ahead in our lives or it would be much easier, or very different. In fact, enjoying the game of life is about knowing how to play the game and daring to participate to the fullest! In the end, we are not playing against one another. However, the goal is for each of us to have a better tomorrow by becoming a progressively better person each day.

The two of us have collaborated on writing what, we feel, are undoubtedly some of the most essential "awesome life" topics. These range from developing and enhancing your skills in Public Speaking, developing a Magnetic Personality to mastering Time Management and Total Health. Ideas and tips to have a Loving Marriage, understanding the value of Meditation, and handling Worry will also be covered. These would not be complete without guidance on Goals, achieving Happiness, attaining Equanimity and the reminder that Life-Long Learning should be the aim of all humans wanting to improve themselves. These topics are among the core concepts required by anyone who desires to achieve that next level of living.

In our attempt to furnish helpful ideas, we have listed several action items at the end of each chapter for your consideration. This is your opportunity to clarify your thinking and take action. Most subjects in life can be boiled down to a few core things you need to know. We believe that the lessons can be learned quickly: in days and weeks rather than years. As with any important undertaking, the real achievement and breakthrough will come when theory ends and consistent forward action begins. Please do the exercises and let us know what you think. We welcome your feedback and look forward to hear about your inspiring stories, as you begin the journey to Awesomeness!

Awesome can be defined in many ways by different people. You are free to define it in any way you want. Here are a few descriptions of awesomeness:

1. *causing feelings of awe and respect,*
2. *something or someone that is extremely good; excellent,*
3. *extremely impressive and inspiring to others.*

The definition most suited for this book is: "Achieving excellence that is impressive, admirable and inspiring." So, are you going to be Awesome?

Why Be Awesome?

For starters, if you are not improving and trying to better yourself, you are slipping behind. Remember this basic fact: there is no neutral or standing still in this life. Everything is either growing or dying. Moving at an average rate puts people in the average category, which results in average results from life, at best. To get awesome results, average goals, average behaviours, average thinking and average efforts will keep the door closed. Why not be awesome instead of average? Why not open the door and break through to a higher level?

People who make little to no effort to improve themselves in life are like a rubber ducky thrown into the sea. They just drift along like flotsam and jetsam in the vast ocean of existence. They can neither steer nor swim, dive nor fly. In fact, they take no active approach to life. They leave things up to fate or destiny. Such people are just plastic objects that can be swallowed up and spit out later if they don't get blown by wind and sea. Or they are tossed onto some random shore to ultimately fade away in the sun or be washed away again by the tide.

In contrast, those who actively engage life on a daily basis are like the osprey or **sea hawk**. The sea hawk lives near the sea and has a purposeful existence. He is an excellent hunter, has amazing eyesight, an outer toe that reverses to help hold slippery fish and a heightened sense of direction despite the seemingly endless expanse of water all around him. Just like humans, this bird of prey is found all over the world. This majestic bird is very talented in living its best life with the skills it possesses. The sea hawk chooses when to fly, dive and hunt as well as choosing when to rest. It has a home to return to and a purpose for its existence. This king of birds is an inspiration to all those who study it and is a metaphor for a complete and meaningful life.

Ultimately, this is not a book that assumes that you are dissatisfied with life. Instead, it is a guide for enhancing your satisfaction of life through the topics covered so that you can get to the next level. This book is not about quick-fix solutions. Rather, it offers an approachable program to lead your life in such a way that you maximize its potential. You can skip over topics or jump to the topics that intrigue you the most, but we suggest you read all the chapters at least once to ensure you get the most out of the book. How you choose to use this information is left entirely up to you. We have been on a journey to write this book and we invite you to join us so that together, we change the world.

The choice belongs to you. Why not soar with purpose and majesty like the sea hawk?

Awesome Life

Chapter 1
Goals Make Us Awesome!

"A man's life is what his thoughts make of it."
Marcus Aurelius

"A man is what he thinks about all day long."
Ralph Waldo Emerson

"And everyone has a goal which dominates him; vie, then, with one another in good works. Wherever you be, Allah will bring you all together. Surely, Allah has the power to do all that He wills."
The Holy Qur'an (2:149)

The life you live will be most enjoyed when you are actively pursuing your meaningful goals. Only you can know what they are and decide to act on them. Perhaps the most important aspect of goal achievement is to know what you want in the first place. You need to identify what it is that you most desire in your life. Try to embrace a goal that means the world to you and dominates your thoughts. Only then will you be well on your way to not only achieving the goal but also becoming a better version of yourself for having achieved the goal. We are not usually inspired by a person just because she climbed a mountain, but by what she had to endure and what she became on her way to the top!

Bake a Cake or Climb Mount Everest This Way

If you reflect on how you achieved your goals in the past, you should be able to recognize a certain pattern or a recipe. It goes something like this: Your goal (the thing you want) comes to life in your mind—you begin to think about it daily—you figure out steps you need to take to bring your thought into the real world—you act—you achieve your goal. It's the famous Commit, Act, See strategy. You must be committed to the desired goal in your mind, then act on the steps necessary to achieve the goal and see your results.

The observation is certainly true for all of us. However, what part does your personal effort play versus good timing or luck? You may be thinking too, is it enough to send the message of achieving your goal to the "universe" and wait for the cosmos to respond by creating the conditions that fulfil your goal or purpose in life? The question for those who have a spiritual bent of mind might be, Is my goal reachable on my own or can I achieve the goal more certainly by invoking the help of the Creator of the Universe? As Albert Einstein remarked:

> *"That deep emotional conviction of the presence of a superior reasoning power, which is revealed in the incomprehensible universe, forms my idea of God."*

Let's think for a moment about the impact of God on your goals. Can you reasonably expect a goal to be achieved if it runs contrary to the plans of God? It stands to reason that the goals that you choose to pursue should be in accordance with what you know are wholesome and beneficial for you and your fellow beings. If you choose a goal that is outside this loose definition, you may never see it come to pass no matter how much you conceive, believe and act to achieve. This then, is a prerequisite to achieving your goals. Set up a goal that is good and not questionable. Outside of this, you should not limit your mind or heart towards the achievement of any wholesome goal. Think of the early Muslim scholars and scientists who were no doubt inspired by the verse in the Holy Qur'an:

"In the creation of the heavens and the earth and in the alternation of the night and the day there are indeed Signs for people of understanding, who remember Allah standing, sitting and lying on their sides and ponder over the creation of the heavens and the earth, which impels them to supplicate: Lord, Thou hast not created this without purpose, Holy art Thou!"
Holy Qur'an 3:191-192

It is reported that the mind of Al Biruni—considered one of the greatest scientists of all times—was inspired by this verse! For these luminaries, the discovery of the workings of the universe and the understanding of the human body were goals that were not just lofty but beyond what any human ever achieved in all of history! Nonetheless, they did achieve their goal. At first, the idea took place in their mind and soon became like an obsession. Next, through trial and error, they took actions and finally, they achieved their goal. Now, what else did they do? What would you have done? They must have prayed to God for guidance and help. Their supplications must have been intense and their patience equal in measure. Our pursuit of knowledge and our spiritual life complement each other. As Albert Einstein said:

"Science without religion is lame, religion without science is blind."

The Recipe for Your Goal Cake

So, let's break it down to a few essential ingredients: visualize, believe, plan, act and throughout it all, ask for God's help! As you visualize your goal, try to give your mind a vivid 3D Ultra HD picture of the whole thing. Add detail to what you want and take away distractions and fuzziness that doesn't belong. Let's say your goal is a leaner and more toned physique. Visualize yourself with the smaller waistline, the broader shoulders, and proper- fitting clothes in all the right places. Mix that with the feeling of firm belief that you can change your current body to get to that desired end state. Your desire has to be at the level of an obsession or passionate desire and not just "it would be great if I was slimmer". Forget about being balanced in your life when you are out to achieve a goal. You might remember the last time you achieved an epic goal; you were not balanced in your day-to-day affairs. In order to achieve your goal, something has to go to the wayside. Indeed, the badge worn by a champion golfer is that he hits an unbelievable amount of balls at the practice range each and every day. Those days and hours of practice are not what you would call a balanced life, but it is the price to pay if the dream of winning a tournament is the goal.

The light-hearted effort will usually not bring results. How obsessed are you with achieving your goal? Does your goal dominate your thoughts? Are you a "dedicated achiever" who is dominated by his or her goal? The thought that you might fail should actually not be in your mind. What should be in your mind is that if you stumbled, would you get up and continue to try? Successful individuals have an unshakeable level of self-confidence and they don't entertain thoughts of leaving the playing field. Not once, not ever! In their hearts, they are focused on the rewards of achieving their goal and are willing to do the work. In their mind, they are setting a higher standard and are willing to pay the price to achieve it. They are willing to fail, be ridiculed, face hardship, hit the wall of doubt, move through uncomfortable change, and be tenacious every day. These are people who remind themselves of how they will feel if they don't try. They would rather face opposing winds in the pursuit of their goal than sit on the sidelines of life.

You can certainly attain what you desire, as the Second

Caliph of Islam—Umar ibn Khattab—relates that he heard the Prophet Muhammad (peace be upon him[1]) say:

> *"Motive determines the value of all conduct, and a person attains that which he desires. If the motive of one who emigrates is to attain to Allah and His Messenger, then that is the purpose of his migration; and he who migrates seeking the world attains to it, and he who migrates for the sake of a woman, marries her and thus his migration is for the purpose he has in mind."*
> (Imam Bukhari and Imam Muslim[2])

After intense visualization, you need to really believe you can achieve your goal. This is the right time to bring out your prayer mat. Connect with your Creator to solidify your belief with intense concentration in prayer. God is your guide and helper. Believing you can do something is half the battle. From the Bible we read:

> *"As a man thinketh in his heart so he is."*
> Proverbs 23:7

We also get this gem of advice too:

> *"And all things, whatsoever ye shall ask in prayer, believing, ye shall receive them."*
> Matthew 21:22

---

[1] It is common practice for Muslims to invoke peace and blessings of God whenever the name of the Prophet Muhammad is mentioned. In writing, it is commonly indicated by placing a superscript such as [pbuh] (meaning: peace be upon him).

[2] Imam Bukhari and Imam Muslim are two of the most authentic narrators of the Traditions of the Prophet Muhammad[pbuh].

Have faith in your belief that you can do what you need to do. However, dare to blend that intense belief with repeated heartfelt prayer and be eagerly prepared to receive what you pray for, God willing! You might also like to think of yourself as the author of the book about your life since we all choose many aspects of the various "chapters" of our lives. As the author of your personal book titled *My Awesome Life*, you can write how your story will play out. Why not write out a great beginning, an exciting middle and a triumphant ending?

Break a Record and Watch Out for Glass Ceilings

Many years ago, Roger Bannister did the unimaginable feat of running a mile in under four minutes. He must have done so by believing he could do it, even though no other human being ever clocked such a superhuman result. Funny thing though, once he was the first to crack the four minute mile a large number of people did the very same thing immediately after he demonstrated that it could be done. The belief that it could be done was all that these other runners needed. It is said that if you put a flea in a jar with a lid on it, the flea will try to jump out as it hits its head at the top of the jar; after a few escape attempts and a sore head, the flea will not jump out of the jar, even once the lid is lifted off. Don't let anyone put a lid over you. A famous Japanese saying is, "*Fall down seven times; get up eight.*" Believe in yourself and your God-given abilities to achieve great things.

Ask Someone Who Has Done It

What next? You need a plan. In some cases, you may be blazing a new trail and no one has done what you are out to do, so go ahead and be the first! However, most goals can be planned by doing one simple thing: find someone who has achieved the thing that is your goal and copy his or her plan. A personal example is getting advice from someone who has written multiple books on how to write a book. The advice we received from published authors was like finding a key to a lock. The time trying to reinvent the wheel was saved and the process became as easy as following a recipe for boiling water. In fact, trying to achieve a goal without identifying someone who has achieved that goal and mimicking their approach, is not helpful to your cause. As the 13th century Muslim mystic, Jalaluddin Rumi, says:

> *"Whoever travels without a guide needs two hundred years for a two-day journey."*

Look at people around you and just ask them the simple question: How did you do it? Listen carefully, make notes and implement the key action steps needed to achieve the similar goal. Offer to take them out for coffee or lunch so that you can learn from them. You will find that such people are willing to share and pay forward mainly because they too once asked a mentor for help.

Strengthen Your Resolve

This is where you need to climb the last stretch to the peak of the mountain. **You** are the only one who can get off the cloud of dreaming about something and get busy implementing. You have a clear vision of what you want; you believe that you can do it; you have a precise roadmap to follow and all that is left to do is doing it! Your level of motivation will take you far, your habits no doubt will help too, your mindset will make a difference indeed; however, nothing will help you as much as prayer to the Almighty for success! Start your goal achievement with a prayer. During your toil, pray some more. When you are fifteen steps away from the top of your own Mt. Everest, and the exhaustion of each step and laboured breath is overwhelming, ask God to carry you to the top!

You might be thinking for a moment that you know lots of people who do not ask God for help and yet they are super-successful. This is not a surprise or a point that should astonish you. In God's grace and kindness, even those who do not ask Him for express help may achieve success, so that in their minds and hearts, the awareness of a Higher Power being present is firmly rooted. Besides, their focus, concentration, planning and declarations are types of prayer, are they not? Ask many such people and they will often credit a Higher Power for carrying them to the finish line! Maybe, at some future point in their lives, they will reflect and know in every fibre of their being that their efforts were assisted by an Invisible Hand—the Great Architect of the Universe.

What to Do if You Face an Obstacle on the Road to Damascus?

Now that we have identified the formula for success, let's examine the main obstacle. It is discipline or lack of it that results in the fire of motivation going out. This is a big problem. As Gautama Buddha taught:

"To conquer oneself is a greater feat than conquering a thousand men in battle".

All that stands between you and your goal might just be you! Many times we are in our own way of achieving a goal and even harming its development because we lack discipline.

This reminds us of a story of campers who made an African safari. As the night approached, they set up their tents and made a fire to stay warm. The safari leader put the campers on a rotating schedule to keep the fire burning bright all night. Everyone falling asleep would mean certain peril. Among the campers, one person asked why they needed to keep the fire burning at all costs. The leader replied, "When the fire goes out, the predators come in!" Are you keeping your fire of motivation burning bright? How do you ensure that it does?

If it were easy to get to the top of your goal mountain, everyone would be reaching it. It's actually quite challenging at times. That's why the world heavyweight boxing champion Muhammad Ali said:

> *"I hated every minute of training, but I said, 'Don't quit. Suffer now and live the rest of your life as a champion.'"*

What did Muhammad Ali actually say? He definitely was clear, but what principle did he highlight with this famous gem of wisdom? Let's call this principle of action "Obsessive Reward Pursuit". Wouldn't you agree that Mr. Ali was in pursuit of being the heavyweight champion of the world and that he was obsessive about it? In fact, he was willing to put up with the discomfort of training hard, when others were enjoying their lives, in order to really enjoy his life and have the comfort of achieving his goal? Perhaps we could all ask ourselves the question that Mr. Ali must have asked himself: "What do I want my future to look like?" After painting a vivid picture and knowing the actions needed to achieve the dream result, you have to be willing to pay the price! You have to be obsessive about reaching your goal. You need to be consumed by it when you are awake and when you dream at night.

That would mean studying one hour longer to score a great exam result. That would mean skipping the chocolate cake at the coffee shop. That would mean eating clean six days a week. That would mean asking people to do business with you and hearing no, more often than yes. That would mean quitting a habit like smoking could be as easy as focusing on the health you will achieve and that you would be willing to face the discomfort of withdrawal for two or three weeks. In fact, the day you really think about avoiding cancer and heart disease, the decision to quit smoking will be easy and putting up with the discomfort of quitting will become bearable. Any time you might feel like lighting up, you would interchange the visual picture of dying in a hospital, weighing eighty-five pounds, hooked up to tubes and having your wife and children next to your bed crying, with the contrasting picture of you looking young, feeling sprightly, and playing with your children's children. You will not light up because you will be in an automatic **obsessive reward pursuit** of living longer and healthier. Could you not achieve any goal by modelling the quit smoking thought process just described?

The real goal achiever is someone who continues to toil long after the initial burst of enthusiasm to lose weight, start a new business or change a disempowering mental habit, passes. He reminds himself of the comfort of being healthier and living a higher quality of life; he reminds himself of the comfort of being his own boss and earning an unlimited amount of money, he reminds himself of the comfort of unshackling himself from pessimistic thinking and living life with joy and celebration! However, in order to achieve his goals, he is willing to endure any level of discomfort to be victorious. He is willing to pay the price to be a champion.

Go Back to the Drawing Board

Sometimes, the goal looks unreachable so consider this: is it the goal or the approach to the goal that is at fault? According to Confucius:

"When it is obvious that the goals cannot be reached, don't adjust the goals, adjust the action steps."

Just as Thomas Edison kept reworking his invention of the light bulb 10,000 times, you too might need to reconsider what you are doing and go back to the drawing board. Most people give up after a few tries. Very few people stick with a goal after nine failures, let alone 9,999 failures. So how do people like Thomas Edison keep on going?

The Rocket Fuel of Goal Achievement

As just mentioned, a monumental goal is usually achieved by staying on purpose long after the initial burst of excitement to attain the goal passes. The moment we feel stuck or know that our motivation has taken a nose dive, we need to remind ourselves of our **why**! In other words, we need to remind ourselves of the 'motive' in our 'motivation'. Make sure that this **why** is not a small one; rather, it must be a **gigantic why**, with the height of the CN Tower and the width like the base of the Rocky Mountains. A father who wants to get in shape and lose weight might remind himself of his reason (**why**) for pursuing his goal in the first place—to be healthy for his children so that he can attend their weddings and be there to help them grow up. A businessman may like to reaffirm his desire to create wealth not just for himself but also for his employees and their families. A student may be feeling run-down during exams and need to remind herself of the prize of entering university, and getting a job that few people on the planet can ever have! Someone might be feeling too lazy to floss his teeth, then remind himself that three cavities cost $600 to fix and having teeth in your forties is a good thing. Know your why, remind yourself of your why and keep the predators out!

To achieve your goal, you will face challenges and doubts. Your desire to continue on will need to be placed upon the jewelled crown of steadfastness, that is, to be committed, unwavering, solid in your resolve, and firm in your faith. As we are reminded in the following Tradition of the Prophet Muhammad[pbuh]:

> *Sufyan ibn Abdullah relates: I asked the Messenger of Allah: Tell me something about Islam which should enable me to dispense with having to ask anyone else. He said: "Affirm: I believe in Allah; and then be steadfast."* (Imam Muslim)

Visualize Your Goals

To remain focused on your **why,** you might like to do an arts and crafts project called a **Personal Goal Poster**. On a poster sized Bristol board or cork board, collect pictures that remind you of your goal and also written messages or headlines, such as slogans, quotes or poems. The finished Personal Goal Poster will be your unique creation and have a meaning to you that is in line with your values and aspirations. You might find pictures in old magazines or newspapers and you might type and print great quotes or clip those, too, from magazines. Frame the finished Personal Goal Poster and take a picture of it on your phone to look at daily and further remind you of this visual tool.

The purpose of your Personal Goal Poster is to look at it often. You need to have it in a place that you pass several times a day. An excellent place might be in your bedroom, or above your desk or in the hallway of your home. Look at it. Be inspired. Think and concentrate on the images and messages. Allow your mind to perform its magic by moving you towards the achievement of the things you aspire to on your poster. Examples might be of a home you would like to own, pictures of those whom you admire for their achievements, a saying from a Holy Book, a quote from a sports legend whom you deeply respect, a short poem from a long-forgotten author. Let the Personal Goal Poster be your visual reminder. Spend two or three minutes daily to stare and focus on one or two things on the poster. Let the subconscious imprint received in your mind activate you to the achievement of the images.

Good Habits, Good Results; Bad Habits...

Another stepping-stone that is needed is to understand that what you get is a **result**. For example, the weight and physique you have today is a result of your current lifestyle and diet. The job or level of business you do is a result of your education, training and habits. Often, this truth can escape us and yet it is true. To break out towards a better result, you will have to give up something (read habit). Perhaps, it is associating with certain types of people (toxic and negative comes to mind), watching excess amounts of TV, or sitting around surfing the Web, constantly checking what's happening in the world. In other words, no true achievement of a goal can be had while letting useless pursuits crowd out the time and attention you may need to work on your goals. As Aristotle noted:

> *"We are what we repeatedly do. Excellence, then, is not an act, but a habit."*

The Focusing Question to Propel You to Your Awesomeness

Do you feel that you have a goal that you have been putting off for months, if not years? Maybe, you have a few goals that you will get to "someday". This type of thinking leaves us casually pursuing our goals. If you think about the time you might have left to achieve your goals, you might think you always have "tomorrow". Somehow, we tend to think that we are going to live forever. We know this is not true and yet we live like tomorrow is a given. We live as though the clock of time will tick for us forever. We often ignore the reality of how limited our existence is. If we live a long life, it might still be considered a short while! What is 62 years? What is 78 years? What is 97 years? Think about this: if you live another thirty years that amounts to exactly 10,950 days. Don't waste a day!

So here is the focusing question to ask yourself and answer: **If you knew you had only two to five years left to live, what direction would you move your life towards, so that you would not have any regrets?** You might want to contemplate the last day of your life and think of the regrets you might have. What might you do right now so that these regrets never occur? Make a list of these regrets: Regret One and have a plan to fix it. Regret Two and have a plan to fix it. Regret Three and have a plan to fix it. We hope you don't have a long list. All you have to do is get going on your goals; don't wait another day or minute. There is magic in believing in yourself and your goals. As the Lord says in The Bhagavad Gita[3]:

> *"When a person is devoted to something with complete faith, I unify his faith in that. Then, when his faith is completely unified, he gains the object of his devotion"*

[3] Literally meaning The Song of the Lord, the Bhagavad Gita is a 700-verse poem in the Sanskrit language and is part of the Indian epic, Mahabharata. The poem is essentially a dialogue between Prince Arjuna and Lord Krishna.

Is Your Fate Predestined?

Now, some of you may be thinking that the achievement of a goal is really predestined and so trying to do something on one's own is futile. This type of thought may be coming to you if you come from a culture that says "God Willing" or as Muslims say *Inshaa-Allah*! We could call this the *Inshaa-Allah Paradox,* if you will. Of course, your Creator knows all and knows the outcome of everything before it happens. Not even a leaf falls to the ground of which God is not aware. That said, we should also think about the actual meaning of this quality of God's omniscience as it relates to knowledge of the future. Indeed, God knows the limits and boundaries of a person's life and achievements but that does not mean that we, as individuals, must resign ourselves to a perceived "destiny" and not try to achieve our goals.

Here is a simple example: God knows that a particular person may live to be 80 years old. That person however, does exercise some influence on this outcome, to the extent that he lives a healthy lifestyle and works within the rules of the laws of nature. If the person does things to promote his health, his life might be lived to the fullest degree, however long it may be. Likewise, by abusing his own health, the person plays roulette and may not live to the range set by God for that person. From the Holy Qur'an we read:

> *"And man will have nothing but what he strives for."*
> Holy Qur'an (53:40)

A blind belief in predestination would have us all living in the Stone Age, let alone the horse and buggy age. Why bother figuring out anything if we are bound to get what we are going to get or be who we are going to be? On the contrary, God made Nature intriguing to man and gave him the faculties of reason and thought to try and study its workings. These innate qualities in all human beings, allows them to have an awareness of the Creator and also the ability to study the various sciences that have given birth to all sorts of technology and gadgets. Consider, for instance, the ability to email a person on the other side of the world on a book-sized computer, weighing barely three pounds! In other words, the nature of man is to strive for a goal and to be bold and figure things out. Commit, Act and See your results. The alternative is to live a passive life of ignorance and unused potential. Robert Louis Stevenson, the Scottish novelist and author of *Treasure Island* and *Strange Case of Dr. Jekyll and Mr. Hyde*, who lived a brief life of forty-four years, wrote:

> *"The world has no room for cowards. We must all be ready somehow to toil, to suffer, to die. And yours is not the less noble because no drum beats before you when you go out into your daily battlefields, and no crowds shout about your coming when you return from your daily victory or defeat."*

Positive Thinking is not Enough!

Now having recognized that your natural position in life is to achieve your mind's desire in all things good, why is it so hard? Many people grow frustrated and quit. Others try a few times and give up. The issue can be resolved if we have a clean mirror and act like farmers and miners. Here is what we mean: if you have a mirror that is smudged and a bit greasy, the image of your face will not be clear. You need to clean that mirror with some glass cleaner and make it clear. Now, what a difference! Same mirror, but your image is clear. Similarly, a person has to dust off any unclear thoughts and see a clear image in the mirror of one's mind—a clear awareness of your thoughts. Cleaning that mirror regularly is like thinking positively. For positive thinking to work, you've got to think positively often and then take positive action too! Very frequently! Several times a day would come close to enough. As Muhammad Ali has said:

> *"It's the repetition of affirmations that leads to belief. And once that belief becomes a deep conviction, things begin to happen."*

This clear image may take time to materialize with your physical eyes and this is what the farmer teaches us. As you know, a farmer plants his crop and has one goal in mind and that is to harvest a bountiful crop. However, he must work hard without letting up, each and every day for weeks and months before he even sees the slightest sign of progress. Days go by and the farmer just sees dirt. Weeks go by and he just sees sprouts. The prize is not instant but he knows that he must toil to get the reward. He can't skip even one step of tilling, watering, fertilizing the earth if he wants the prize. It is through his unwavering persistence that he claims a harvest! You too must be that persistent. In the Holy Qur'an we read:

> *"Allah is with the steadfast."*
> Holy Qur'an (2:245)

Rome was not built in a day and neither will the achievement of your goal.

One has to do all the little things and not give up three feet away from striking gold. Some people give up or lose hope and others dig a little deeper, like a determined gold miner; they keep at it and they are the ones that strike the vein of gold. So be a farmer and a miner and just show up every day to do the work! And of course, pray for success and the courage you need to never give up. Be encouraged when you read in the Holy Qur'an:

> *"Verily he truly prospers who purifies himself."*
> Holy Qur'an (87:15)

You were meant to prosper! Positive thinking and positive actions combined with prayer is truly a transformative power! Recruit these thoughts and ask God to be your partner in all your endeavours! Keep busy thinking forward. And remember this statement made by William Gladstone, the Victorian-era British Prime Minister:

> *"No man ever became great or good except through many and great mistakes."*

Indeed, by doing things and learning from our missteps, we actually get to the ultimate goal of becoming better versions of ourselves and masters of our destiny.

Action Steps

1. Write down at least one point in this chapter that really resonates with you.

2. Outline three life goals that you must achieve but you have been putting off for too long.

3. List the plan you think you need to achieve these goals.

4. Highlight the first step you need to take to get started. Just begin. View any failure as feedback; do not quit!

5. Develop the mindset that you are a diamond in the rough and that you will polish yourself and are only limited by yourself. Remind yourself that you can go as far as your mind will take you!

6. Make a list of 25 things about yourself that are awesome! An example could be: I am a good friend; I am a great communicator; I am creative; I have great habits etc. This list will put you in a frame of mind that will boost your confidence level. Confidence is a great confidence booster! Introduce this idea to your kids; have them type it out and frame it to be viewed in their bedroom. Offer them $25 to complete the project. From confidence comes a Can Do attitude.

7. Decide how you will keep the fire going to motivate you to achieve your goal. One way is to pursue what interests you. When you are interested in something, pursuing it becomes a pleasure, not a pain.

8. Enlist one or more friends to help you work through your goals.

9. List names of two or more people who inspire you and state which actions or habits of theirs that you might adopt.

10. Answer the question: How will I feel one year from now, if I don't get started on my goals?

Chapter 2
Time Investment

"The key is in not spending time, but in investing it."
Stephen R. Covey

"Dost thou love life? Then do not squander time, for that's the stuff life is made of."
Benjamin Franklin

"Time is really the only capital any human being has and the only thing he can't afford to lose."
Thomas Edison

We are all here for a limited time. Your time is valuable, especially the older you get. There is much to do before we get to the final act. We are reminded of this in Psalms 90:12:

"So teach us to number our days that we may get a heart of wisdom."

In a practical sense, we all have the same amount of hours in a day. What matters is how we use our time and in that respect, we are all unique. So, to best use our time at any given moment, we should be asking ourselves the following question: **"What is the best use of my time, right now?"** Time management is not a matter of managing time as much as it is of managing ourselves and using ideas and techniques to make the best use of our time. The three main points we will consider are, Time Investment, Attention Management and Project Planning. We will take a look at each of these points in this chapter.

First, what is Time Investment and why bother? The three quotes above say it all, don't they? Have you noticed that the successful people of the world in any field of life have achieved great things because of the way they spent their time? When you think of it, time is truly an investment (giving one valuable thing to gain an even more valuable thing). Consider how we regularly exchange time for knowledge all through school life. Later, we exchange time for money when we get a job or run a business. Depending on how much time we invest and the return on investment in terms of knowledge, money or happiness achieved, we consider this either a good use of our time or time wasted. Anything we want to achieve involves an investment of time, so rather than trying to manage the hours and minutes in a day, we all need to figure out *what* is worth pursuing and *how much* time needs to be invested to achieve it.

Invest in your Most Critical Activities

So, how should we decide to invest our time? It can be challenging, but not complicated when you look through the right lens. You need to start by figuring out the **Most Critical Activities** (MCAs) for each day. These are things that will help you achieve your goals and are congruent with your deepest values. Every day, ask yourself: **"What are the two or three Most Critical Activities that must get done today?"** These are activities that define your day. These are not activities that would be "nice to do" or you "wish you had time for". These are the absolute must do things before you can go to bed that evening! Once you define these, it's easier to move forward and actually get things done with the time you invest in a given activity or project.

If you become disciplined enough to define your MCAs each day, you will have better days and actually make measurable progress in life. Just make sure there are no more than three MCAs for each day, the rest can be "nice to do" or wish-list items. These non-MCA things can be ignored or postponed until the MCAs are done. This simple habit and self-limitation on the total number of MCAs, gives you much needed focus for each day. You can also achieve your plan for the next day, if you make a list of your next day's MCAs at the end of the day. Rather than leave your desk at quitting time, spend five minutes creating a new list of three MCAs for tomorrow. This way you hit the ground running the next day and don't end up wasting time figuring out what to do first.

Pay Attention to What's Important

Now that you have your MCAs mapped out and you know where to invest your time, it's time to manage your attention. Why? Because we need to give attention to these high payoff MCAs, so we can progress towards our goals. Time is squandered when our attention is not focused. The day before you leave for a vacation is usualfy your most productive day! Focusing your attention will also help you from falling victim to the OOPS (Overly Optimistic Planning Syndrome) system of time management. Guard your attention by avoiding interruptions with a closed door and a sign outside that signals you are focusing. We all know what it's like to be in a groove and then have someone or something interrupt our train of thought. Just getting back and starting again takes added time and finding that "attention" again is not easy. We are surrounded by distractions and on top of that, everyone is telling us that we need to multi-task and get "more" done. After defining your MCAs for the day, you have taken the first step to managing your attention, because you know that whatever is an MCA needs attention; the rest can be parked. What about the **To Do** items not on your MCA list? Ignore them. Just stop thinking about them and free your mind as well as your time.

Detox Your Life to Focus your Attention

Your body is not the only thing that needs a detox. When you are serious about being focused, you would be wise to unplug from TV, Internet, music and social pressure while you are completing your MCAs. Tell yourself that they don't matter until the MCAs are done. If you are watching TV or a movie when you should be working on your MCAs (read Goal Achievement Behaviour), you might remind yourself that the folks you are watching were well-compensated to act in the show, while you are not moving towards your goals. When it's time to work, you should work. When it's time to play, by all means watch a well-deserved TV show or do whatever else floats your boat.

Another way to detox your life and make room to focus your attention is to learn to say **no** more often. Remember, you are on a mission to get things done that are important to you and that move you towards achieving your goals. So, when someone pops into your life asking you to do something that is not part of your MCAs, it's okay to say no. Say it nicely and stay true to your overall principles of life. You will instantly get more done of those things that matter to you. Your default should be to say **no** to most things seeking your attention and have a compelling reason, before you say **yes** to something. If not giving a flat no, ask **why** to everything, to see if it makes sense to do that thing competing for your attention. Many people would like to have your attention so that they can achieve their goals, but how does that help you? Some people, who do not value time, like to waste others' time to fill their own. You, on the other hand, are better off if you avoid this and stay focused on your own objectives. Do you think that someone can waltz in to the office of a Prime Minister and waste her time? Why should anyone or anything do that to you? Are you also not important?

Don't Go After Vain Pursuits

We must be strict with our time since it is the most precious of the limited resources we have. We should be guarding it like a treasure. No one is going to give us more time or to slow it down for us to "get things done". We have to push things off our table if they are not truly important to our lives, and not moving us towards the achievement of our goals. There are plenty of people in the world who will 'donate' their attention and energy to advertisements, Internet surfing, social media and various forms of entertainment. Let that not be you. The world of business, organizations and people are all vying for your valuable time and attention. Give it to them when it is most appropriate and in the right quantity. Your life will be better once you live life on your terms rather than living through the temptations and distractions of what others want you to be doing.

The following two quotes are great reminders of how we might treat vain and useless distractions that surround us. Not everything needs our immediate attention or response. Our own respect for our valuable time requires that we not indulge in trivial matters. From the Holy Qur'an we read:

> *"And those who bear not false witness, and when they pass by anything vain, they pass on with dignity;"*
> Holy Qur'an (25:73)

> *"And when they hear vain talk, they turn away from it and say, 'Unto us our works and unto you your works. Peace be to you. We seek not the ignorant.'"*
> Holy Qur'an (28:56)

A major source of vanity and one of today's biggest time wasters is social media. It helps to simply not use

Facebook or Twitter. If you don't have them, you won't have any pressure to keep checking them for updates. Email and phone texts consume a startling amount of time too. Living totally without email might not be reasonable, but certainly setting up a routine to check it three times a day is reasonable. Truly urgent information will show up as a phone call and the world will keep revolving! True, we all need to unwind with our favourite activities be they social media, watching TV and so on; however, these things should be treated like a reward rather than an everyday mindless routine or compulsion. Certain folks reading this book will remember what life was before cellphones. Today, everyone it seems has a cellphone. Somehow, this device needs to be renamed because it is so much more than a phone. Cellphones are not phones anymore; they are a gateway to the world outside your immediate world and present a constant source of tapping on your shoulder. Start by turning off your phone or putting it in another room while you are cranking out an MCA. Every bleep and beep can be passed on with dignity.

De-Clutter Your Workspace

Many of the things we think are important are just useless distractions that we have lived without for centuries. Just as distractions from gadgets, media, Internet and so on make our mental and emotional environment messy, so does physical clutter. It's best to clear your workspace so that you have a clean surrounding and state of mind to start and finish things. Each day you sit at your workspace or study desk, start by asking yourself how many things are truly needed on your desk and subtract them one by one until you have only the things you require daily. Everything else can go in a drawer, be discarded through recycling or given away to someone who may need that item. This will help you to focus your attention and get the MCA items done.

Never Chase Two Rabbits at One Time

The precious value of being in the moment is important to your use of time just as much as it is to enjoying your life:

"Do not dwell in the past; do not dream of the future; concentrate the mind on the present moment."
Buddha

So, whenever you are faced with something important that you need to take action on and it only needs two to five minutes of time, do it right away with complete focus. For your longer projects, you might like to develop a single-tasking philosophy: stay with the project for the allotted time and stay on task. Trying to do multiple tasks or mixing simple and complex tasks will result in both being done poorly, if you complete either one at all! Studies have shown that there is no such thing as effective multi-tasking for most people. We are just not wired to reliably do two or more things at once; why try? Furthermore, multi-tasking actually drains our mental and physical energy and fools us into thinking we are doing more work with less time or energy. In reality, we may at best become very good at attention switching and at worst, ignore key information which could lead to death—think of texting and driving as an example. Some of the best accomplishments by the greatest artists, statesmen or captains of industry were not done while texting someone on the phone, watching TV or surfing the web. An old saying captures the importance of this:

"If you don't have time to do it right, make time to do it over again".

You might like to frame this quote and place it on your desk to remind you not to multi-task. You are an important and busy person and you know that you don't have time to do things over again.

"To do two things at once is to do neither."
Publius Syrus

This centuries-old quote is another great reminder against multi-tasking. Obviously, single-tasking is not a trending topic of our modern day; however, it's simply good for you. By focusing on one task, you will get more done with better-quality results. If you finish early, you can plan for the next single-tasking activity and finish ahead of schedule. From this victorious position, you should continue the pattern for the rest of your work day. This is natural for most of us and gives us the ability to truly concentrate on one thing. It also means your mind is not racing in multiple directions because you have a habit of always being in multi-tasking mode. Being in a constant frantic and rushed state may lead to increased stress, burnout and difficulty sleeping—something that you do not want to invite into your life. Single-tasking makes a lot of sense, just like reading one book at a time and finishing it, rather than starting six different books at the same time and ending up finishing none.

Focus on Working Less to Get More Done

Some people have jobs that cause them to sit for hours on end. We can easily get so caught up in our work that time is distorted and by sitting for multiple hours, one becomes a victim of their intense focus. A great idea is to set a timer or some alarm that goes off after 45 minutes of quality work. When the alarm goes off, leave the chair and change your setting by leaving your work space to take a 10 to 15-minute break. By doing this, you will stay alert and be even more productive. This will be better for your overall health too, if you have a sitting job, since you will be getting up to stretch every hour and therefore stay fresh. Yes, that's what the 15-minute breaks are for, rather than checking your Facebook or Twitter updates or surfing the Web. If you were to take a 15-minute break each hour you will end up taking a total of 1 hour and 45 minutes of break time on top of a one-hour lunch, effectively leaving you a bit over five hours to get your work done.

This habit of taking more breaks might seem like you will shortchange yourself in terms of time available to get things done. This will be true if you do not focus during your work time; however, you will get more done when you know you have less time to do it in. As a rule, work expands to the time allotted. If you give yourself one hour to finish a task, that's how long it will take. If you give yourself 45 minutes, that's how long it will take, plus you can take a break where you can stretch your legs, clear your mind or drink some refreshing water. Withdrawing from the world does not have to happen once in a while; it can easily happen five times a day. You could use these breaks for soul-nourishing quiet time, introspection, prayer or even meditation. Just don't get yourself wound up or entangled in some adrenaline-pumping distraction.

Plan Your Day and Work Your Plan

Have you ever had a day where you spent the full day doing "work" but actually got very little done? How does that happen? Where does the time go? Why can't everyday be a super-productive day? Here is where time-blocking and getting on a roll makes a lot of sense. If you know your MCA is to call your top clients, rather than call them as time permits, you could make a time block where all you do is make outgoing calls from 10 a.m. to noon, for example. During this time, you would not check emails or take incoming calls. You certainly would not chat with a co-worker who drops in or become distracted in any way whatsoever. This will create your "roll" and each call you make will be impactful and dynamic because you will be in a rhythm. The less you allow one task to merge into the other, the more satisfaction and achievement you will experience. You will also have fewer things to do over, fix, re-learn or understand for the first time.

In other words, when you work, you should work the plan that you create for yourself each day. Distractions are the enemy—they were thirty years ago and they will be thirty years from now. The current suspects of email, incoming calls, addictive TV shows, gaming, social media updating and checking, and various other fun things in life can be delayed, recorded and reviewed later. Life is happening in real time and we can't rewind or replay moments. So it's better to be in the moment as much as possible and see what is happening, as it happens. This enriches you and your ability to use time to your advantage. Don't be one of the masses; determine your quality of life and rise to the level you feel you deserve. Act on your own plan, not the plan or expectation of anyone else.

Life As a Series of Projects

The third thing we need focus on is planning and completing our projects. So what's the difference between a task and project? A task is a simple activity that achieves a single and usually small goal like taking out the garbage, ironing clothes, watering plants or making a phone call. A project, on the other hand, is a more complex and larger goal with multiple tasks required to achieve it, such as moving, getting married, studying for exams, completing a course project, completing a proposal at work or planning a trip. Projects can take days, months or years to achieve, but we can break them down into smaller action items that we can execute in hours, days or weeks.

Project planning means: mapping out the short-term (one to three months) and long-term (one to five years) goals and also breaking down the steps for each of these. The project steps should be identified with one- month outlines and weekly specific steps. In other words, even though your project (for example, writing a book) may take two years to complete, you need to identify what you will do over the upcoming month and break that down into weekly actions. Naturally, you will be executing daily actions, but you must check in weekly to make sure you are tracking towards completion of the plan. Otherwise, a week will go by wasted. We've all been there. With this system, you have no excuse and will get your "projects" done. One by one, your dreams will manifest and you will astonish yourself. As someone very wise said, "Inch by inch, it's a cinch!"

We can also tell our friends, family and others about our projects to help keep some positive pressure on us. Due to the duration of the projects in life, you will often need someone who is dedicated to keeping you accountable throughout the project. It is a good idea to establish and maintain a link with someone who becomes your coach. This person is there to check in regularly on how you are progressing, help you work through problems or hurdles and generally help to motivate you to complete the projects. If necessary, they can also help you to alter the project to make it better. Find people in your life that could help you in this way and also consider those outside your network of family and friends. Likewise, be willing to share your time and experience with others who may be working on their own life projects, for which you could be an ideal coach. Don't be surprised when you start completing projects with ease and start becoming a person of action!

Marvellous Maryam Manages Herself

Maryam used to show up every day of her life hoping the day would go well. She was often playing ping-pong on a daily basis, that is, she was the ball and other people in her life were holding the ping-pong paddles. She was often frustrated by feelings of being out of control and of falling behind on her projects. She also knew that her highest values and purpose in life were falling to the wayside, because her time was being wasted in one way or another. One day, after feeling a bit run-down and haggard, she vowed to not let another day go by without improving herself. She felt intuitively that she needed to manage herself better so that time would be managed automatically. She realized that everyone had the same amount of time available to them, but that some people knew how to act and get more out of each waking hour.

She started to identify her MCAs and began abandoning the notion of multi-tasking; she took strategic breaks throughout her day and found that her day was not as boring or structured when she focused on a few important things. She found it to be quite the opposite, because she could take care of the necessary things each day. This left her time to schedule in some fun as well. Her time was spent executing strategic actions for her tasks or projects. Completing these gave Maryam feelings of accomplishment and great satisfaction, and brought a sense of calm and mastery to her work.

Who Does That?

Some of these suggestions might seem onerous and unrealistic. Many people run their lives based on instinct versus structure and systems. To answer the question, Who does that? Not very many people—and that is why you can be sure you are on to something. In general, there are seven reasons why not everyone uses structure and systems to organize their lives:

1. Most people are comfortable and don't want to change.
2. Most people don't want to put in the extra effort.
3. Most people are afraid of personal commitment.
4. Most people don't lead a purpose-guided life.
5. Most people don't have a consciously-designed life.
6. Most people don't research means and ways.
7. Most people don't act on their good ideas.

The benefits of all these suggestions go beyond simple time management. You can expect better sleep, lower stress, and a real sense of accomplishment at the end of each day. Check things off your list and feel good about it. By deciding what an MCA is, and focusing your undivided attention on it, you invest your time in the best way. By breaking down the steps of your projects, you invest your time efficiently, too. Consider what you are investing your time in today and manage yourself accordingly, because that will define and shape your present and future outcomes. And remember the words of Walt Disney when you think your work is done:

"Disneyland will never be completed. It will continue to grow as long as there is imagination left in the world."

Action Steps

1. Clearly identify your goals and values.

2. Define your Most Critical Activities (MCAs) for today and act on them for seven days in a row. As Bruce Lee said, "*The successful warrior is the average man with laser-like focus.*"

3. Enlist someone to be your coach and cheerleader.

4. De-clutter your life. Eliminate the watching of news or sports and get off social media completely for one week. Just perform your MCAs for that week.

5. Define your short-term and long-term projects and list the steps to achieving each.

6. Make at least two days each month personal development days to either improve your skills or to develop new ones, so that you are able to accomplish your MCAs and projects with mastery. This will give you 24 days a year to sharpen your abilities!

7. Take a break at least one day a month and do nothing but recreation; remember you are "re-creating" yourself! All work and no play makes Jill a dull girl.

8. Study those in your family and field of interest who are accomplishing their goals, so that you learn how they do it. Do they simply work harder or put in longer hours or do they work smarter? Do they have more focus? Do they try to multi-task throughout their day or do they single-task and accomplish things quicker the first time?

9. Make managing yourself your time management philosophy.

Chapter 3
Magnetic Personality

"If it wasn't for the coffee, I'd have no identifiable personality whatsoever."
David Letterman

"Strive constantly to serve the welfare of the world; by devotion to selfless work, one attains the supreme goal of life. Do your work with the welfare of others always in mind."
The Bhagavad Gita

"Deeds of kindness are equal in weight to all the commandments."
The Talmud

Have you ever walked into a room and just felt the presence of a person? As you greeted that person, there was an energy of genuine connection that was being projected at you and felt by you. These people are just magnetic; they have an other-worldly air about them. When you are in their company, you are drawn to them and when they are away from you, you miss them. Such people make you feel special and give you energy. These people make life enjoyable, especially when they are on your list of friends or in leadership roles. Such people are not easily forgotten.

Your Awesome Personality Unleashed

So how does one go about becoming "well-liked" and admired versus being gritty and abrasive? What makes a magnetic personality? Is it inborn or can it be built? To be well-liked as a friend, a colleague, as a leader or even a parent is a worthwhile goal and will make your life and the life of those around you a state of heaven on Earth.

The method to follow is clear and easy if you try. The first step is to be yourself. You have a unique personality and no one can be you; neither should you be someone else. The second step is to cultivate the higher virtues such as genuine compassion for others. Third, develop an honest interest in others.

Quite frankly, the more you come across as yourself, the more people will feel connected to you and walk away with a feeling that "Hey, I really like that guy". The more you focus on higher virtues versus reactive emotions, the more those around you will respect you. The more you give them the chance to tell their story and what's important to them, the more they will feel that you genuinely appreciate them.

These principles are in accordance with nature and how people feel. As Maya Angelou has remarked:

> *"I've learned that people will forget what you said, people will forget what you did, but people will never forget how you made them feel."*

Think about it. When we meet someone and are interacting with him for any length of time, we are sizing him up and making notes to ourselves about how we feel about him. It is said that you don't get a second chance to make a first impression. How true! Making a lasting first impression comes easily if you focus on the three points just mentioned.

Perhaps, the key to developing a magnetic personality is to be a person who does good to others and brings them benefit without expectation of reward, thanks or ulterior motive. In other words, be nice and helpful seeking nothing in return. It says in the Holy Qur'an:

> *"The reward of goodness is nothing but goodness."*

(55:61)

"And they (the virtuous) feed for the love of Him, the poor, the orphan and the prisoner; assuring them: 'We feed you to win Allah's pleasure only. We desire no reward or thanks from you."
(76:9-10).

"You are the best people raised for the good of mankind; you enjoin what is good and forbid evil..."
(3:111)

We also find in the recorded Traditions of the Prophet Muhammad[pbuh]:

"Anybody who looks after his brother's need, Allah will look after his needs." (Abu Dawud)

Be Genuine and All Will be Well

Such a person who operates on doing favours to get favours in return can only be ever viewed as a "schemer" and never as a "sincere" individual. On the street, you get recognition for being "real" and keeping it real. Be that person who is known as a benefactor to his friends, colleagues, community, and neighbours and you will earn your place in people's hearts. There is an incident from the life of the Prophet Muhammad[pbuh] about an old lady who had come to live in Mecca having heard about the Prophet and wanting to know him. No sooner had she arrived than some people told her to avoid meeting him because he would use magic to overcome her. Thinking of this, she decided to leave Mecca and return home. She started back on her journey carrying the luggage she had brought with her. On route, she met the Prophet Muhammad[pbuh] who offered to carry her load. When they arrived, the old lady wanted to reward him for his kind act. The Prophet Muhammad[pbuh] declined to take anything. She asked him for his name and he replied, Muhammad. She smiled and said that she understood now what "magic" he used, and that it is the magic that God gives to his special people.

Go out of your way to lighten someone's mood, to help someone finish a task, lift her up in some way, help her with some garden work, encourage her and cheer her on. You will feel great and you will be magnetic to others!

Do the Right Thing—Anyway

There is a story about Mother Teresa. When asked whether she would join in a march against war, she declined. But she also said that if they were planning a march for peace, she would be happy to join them. She left us the following admonition:

> *"People are often unreasonable, illogical, and self-centred—forgive them anyway.*
> *If you are kind, people may accuse you of selfish, ulterior motives—be kind anyway.*
> *If you are successful, you will win some false friends and some true enemies—succeed anyway.*
> *If you are honest and frank, people may cheat you—be honest and frank anyway.*
> *What you spend years building, someone could destroy overnight—build anyway.*
> *If you find serenity and happiness, they may be jealous—be happy anyway.*
> *The good you do today, people will often forget tomorrow—do good anyway.*
> *Give the world the best you have, and it may never be enough—give the world the best you've got anyway.*
> *You see, in the final analysis, it is between you and God; it was never between you and them anyway."*

What Is In a Virtue?

In other words, to develop a winning personality you should be focused on cultivating the higher virtues such as calmness instead of anger, kindness instead of selfishness, caring instead of indifference, love instead of hard-heartedness, temperance instead of impetuousness, honesty instead of wickedness, peace-making instead of drama-making, optimism instead of pessimism, cheerfulness instead of irritability, bravery instead of cowardice, gratitude instead of self-absorption, perseverance instead of giving up, self-regulation instead of loss of self-control, forbearance instead of resentment, mercy instead of quick temper, patience instead of impatience, meekness instead of pride, self-reliance instead of entitlement thinking, and trusting in God instead of worry. We will find tremendous instruction in the following verse of the Holy Qur'an, a verse that should not go unnoticed:

"*Verily, he truly prospers who purifies himself.*"
Holy Qur'an (87:15)

And as the Prophet Muhammad[pbuh] taught:

"A brave person is not someone who wins in wrestling rather a brave person is he who controls himself in anger."

In other words, your personality is your character, as has been said by Macduff, in Shakespeare's play *Macbeth*:

"Character is the product of daily, hourly actions, and words and thoughts: daily forgiveness, unselfishness, kindnesses, sympathies, charities, sacrifices for the good of others, struggles against temptations, submissiveness under trial. It is these, like the blending

colours in a picture, or the blending notes of music, which constitute the man."

Consider the example of a young athlete from an industrial town outside Pittsburgh. Today he is an international icon and his name evokes the name of his sport. We know him for his accolades, but what many people do not know is how he reveres his fans and how he makes them feel. Every fan letter that was ever written to him is stored in safe-keeping and every year since he received them, he personally replied. His fans are known as his Army and he always took time to spend time with them and sign autographs. Wondering who he is? He is Arnold Palmer. People don't just love his game and contributions —they love him!

Admired Friend—Explained

Now, if you look at your various roles in life, we can focus on just two and get huge returns on our efforts. First is our role as a friend, and second is our role as a leader. As a friend, we are in a relationship with someone whom we truly value. Spending time with that person makes us feel happy and we can just totally be ourselves. So, if you truly value someone who makes you happy, what obligations and duties do you owe to your friend? Several, you'd surely agree: stay in touch in a real face-to-face way if possible, not just by email, text, Facebook or the occasional phone call. Be there for your friend, not only in the good times but in her tough times; your friendship is a lifetime commitment. Never ditch your friends to be part of a more popular group; you might realize the hard way that your true friends are the ones whom you are leaving, not pursuing. Encourage your friends in their efforts, we all need cheerleaders and accountability buddies! As Ralph Waldo Emerson said:

"To share often and much...to know even one life has breathed easier because you have lived. This is to have succeeded."

Cherish your friends; never take your friends for granted and never treat them without respect. Remember, that a true friend always should tell you what is right whether you like it or not, otherwise, neither of you will improve if he or she only tells you what you want to hear. Just be sure to be considerate when stating the truth and not blunt, hurtful or proud. Even though you may have been friends for years, a bit of tact will always be appreciated.

On the note of developing a strong and lifelong friendship, always be aware of how easily a friendship can break—and not only break, but be impossible to revive. In dealing with each other as friends, we might get put off by something the person did or said that did not meet our expectations. Such occurrences are common and can only be expected. We are all prone to misunderstanding and jumping to conclusions. This takes the form of being sure of what your friend said or did and realizing later that there was more to the story. Here is a quick example: you call your friend to come over to help you move and he says he can't help; you immediately conclude that he does not care about you enough. This thought festers in your mind all day long as you are lifting boxes and as you remember how you helped to paint his house just two weeks ago. The thoughts of "what's going on" are heightened when you stub your toe on a sofa in the middle of the hallway. Meanwhile, "what's really going on" is not what you were creating in your head at all!

What actually happened the night before in your friend's life was a personal crisis that involved his cousin. The crisis had become front and centre for your friend, who had to make a difficult choice of whom to help. Rather than jump to conclusions and stay forever hurt or slighted, give others the benefit of the doubt and even better, clarify. Don't play the game of "What's going on vs. What's really going on". Another way of describing this is that there are really three sides to every situation: the way you see it, the way the other person sees it and then the facts.

Beloved Leader—Explained

As a leader, we have great opportunities to lead and be admired rather than lead and be feared. With the tip of a sword, you might be able to bend someone's head, but you will never win his heart. As a leader you have a choice: be loved or hated. For starters, leave your ego at the door. Whether you are leading a small group at work or you are the CEO of a corporation, you are just a cog in the wheel and you are dealing with other thinking and feeling human beings. Reflect, if you will on the following saying of the Prophet Muhammad[pbuh]:

"The leader of a nation is the servant of them."

What if you genuinely took this advice? What changes would you make? One change might be to do what is in the greater good for all concerned, not just yourself. You might change your language, reminding yourself that you work **with** people, not that people work for you or under you. As a leader, you are actually a servant of those who follow you. Your leadership might be that of a politician, or as a champion of a cause, or as a volunteer at your local food bank, but your role is really the same; you lead by serving, not by being a "boss". The meaning of the above Tradition is that when a leader truly serves the people, only then does she become the true leader whom people will love and respect.

The Better Way to Motivate Others

Every leader has a job to do and it usually requires the whole-hearted cooperation of her team. The type of agreement and results you seek as a leader is real agreement and above-average results. As leader of a team, a company or your kids, try to inspire people when you wish to see results rather than simply giving orders. Let folks know that you believe in them and give them encouragement alongside ideas and instructions. Inspiration can take the form of saying, "This is ideally what needs to get done and I know you can do it." The recipient of this message will feel greater commitment and will try to validate your belief in her. Alternatively, when, as a leader or parent, you simply give orders, you go against human nature, because nobody likes to be told what to do. Be liberal with praise and continuously inspire people to be the best they can be. You will make the person feel great and will cause him to think "Hey, if _______ thinks I can do it, I should give it a try."

Think Twice Before You Speak

Ultimately, you are answerable as a leader and all eyes are on you. With great power comes great responsibility. Most importantly, remember that words are like arrows, that is, once they are released you can't get them back, so think twice before you speak. Choose your words carefully and use the best language to express yourself. It has been said that your words can make you a king or a queen and they can also make you a pauper. You reveal a great deal about yourself when you start speaking to others. People's impression of you is instantly formed based on how you deal with them and how you deal with others. The fact is, if a great leader is gentle with her words and effective by using the right words, everyone around her will be awestruck, especially when work deadlines are approaching and business pressures are bubbling over. No one wants to be labelled a "loose cannon". As a leader, the more grace under pressure you show, the more everyone will salute you.

Two More Solid Tips

Another thing to watch over is to never make disparaging remarks about anyone, no matter what. Do your best to find something to compliment about people around you. These positive remarks will eventually reach the ears of the person complimented. When they do, you will be regarded as a gracious person. Just as important: practice being a good listener. When someone is speaking to you, turn off all other thoughts and mental chatter and really listen! You'll be amazed at how much richer the experience becomes. Be present in the conversation in body and mind.

As a Friend or Leader, Lose This Word!

In conversation, never use the word **but**, because as soon as you say it, you are shutting down the chance of the other person seeing your point. To the person who hears the **but** in your sentence, it's like hearing "I get your point but in fact you are wrong; let me break it down for you, let me show you the superiority of my position and you will see that you are wrong and I am right". Rather than use **but**, use the magic of **and**. Try it. Say what you were going to say and do not use **but**; replace it by **and**. You will be astonished at how it works! You might say, "I understand that you are probably thinking this idea may not work **and** if you just give it a try, you will be pleasantly surprised". **And**, not **but**.

The Power of Cloning Yourself

In the spirit of passing on the mantle of leadership to others, you may like to develop your team members into leaders too. There are many ways to do this: Show them that there are no problems but just opportunities and challenges. Show them that they should accept that others can and will have a different view of the issues than they do. Show them that they ought to remain open to ideas from those on their team. Show them to lead with fairness and integrity. Show them that their reputation will take years to build and minutes to destroy. Show them how to get to know people and their concerns. Show them the benefits of collaborating on ideas and seeking input from all team members. Show them it's better to be pleasant, especially under pressure. Show them that it is best to cultivate a reputation that precedes you and is worthy of mention. Show them by your example.

A great leader will inspire her followers. Set big goals and push your team's potential. Under pressure, a piece of coal becomes a diamond. Your team will thank you. Give them an ideal to aspire to by motivating them and giving them opportunities to soar to a greater height than even you have reached. Get out there and simply encourage others to do well. Teach them that the real meaning of **can't** is Certainly Are Not Trying. Be liberal with praise and be the most positive person in the bunch. Your enthusiasm will become infectious. Don't just instruct but rather, roll up your sleeves. Walk your talk so that you will not be just a leader, but one who is a beloved leader.

Action Steps

1. Do your own personality audit. Could you improve on something? What would that be?
2. Look good, so that you never need that second

chance to make a first impression. Wear your best clothes always. Go to a tailor and have them fitted. Pants that are too long and shoes that are dusty detract from your "personality quotient". Keep groomed and coiffed. Wear a nice perfume or cologne. Why wait for Friday, Saturday or Sunday?

3. Think of your best friend. What about the way they deal with you, do you like? Are you that way with your other friends?
4. As you look around the world today, who inspires you as a leader worth emulating? Study his or her life. What about a person in history?
5. Reconnect with an old friend. Set a date to meet him for lunch, write him an old-fashioned, hand-written letter.
6. Go meet a former manager or teacher or mentor and let her know how much her counsel helped you in your life.
7. Recall an experience where you felt like a great leader. Don't forget it.
8. Which of the Prophets inspire you? Get to be an expert on their "way of being".
9. Look for opportunities to show your friendship, leadership and outstanding personality.
10. Remember that a common quality that underscores and supports these three areas (friendship, leadership and personality) is to be an encourager of people. Up your quantity of praise and encouragement to others. People need it like they need air to breathe.
11. Resolve to be a master of your personality. Get on it; it's a good train!
12. Imagine your funeral—will it be attended by at least forty people? How about three thousand?

Chapter 4
Character—Be the Guy

"Character cannot be developed in ease and quiet. Only through experience of trial and suffering can the soul be strengthened, ambition inspired, and success achieved."
Helen Keller

"I look to a day when people will not be judged by the colour of their skin, but by the content of their character."
Martin Luther King Jr.

"The law of harvest is to reap more than you sow. Sow an act, and you reap a habit. Sow a habit and you reap a character. Sow a character and you reap a destiny."
James Allen

Don't be a Guy Who Knows a Guy—Be the Guy!

What does this quip mean to you? Allow us to offer one possible explanation that might resonate loudly and deeply. We all have someone in our life whom we think of first when help is needed. This person is dependable. This person is a person of action. By and large, these people are quite selfless and decisive too.

If you are asked to get something done, how do you handle it? Do you look to pass it off for someone else to do? Do you make excuses about how you are too busy? Do you complain that it's too hard to do and better left undone? Or do you run with it, take the bull by the horns, figure things out and produce results? What does the world need more of: people who shirk responsibility or those who rise to any and all challenges? Who would you rather hire?

Who would you rather have your back? Who would you feel proud to count as your friend?

One such person in the faded memory of history was named Lieutenant Andrew Rowan. He was sent on an important mission to deliver a message to General Calixto Garcia during the Spanish American War. This task, of extreme importance was commissioned by the President of the United States, William McKinley. General Garcia was somewhere in the jungles of Cuba. No one knew where he was precisely. As soon as Lieutenant Rowan landed at night by boat, he set off with the message strapped to his chest in an oilskin pouch, alone. In what must have been a dangerous and challenging mission, Rowan delivered the message and came out on the other side of the island three weeks later. For his outstanding heroism, he was decorated with the Distinguished Service Cross. Lieutenant Rowan was undoubtedly a man of action. He was not the type to pass on his duty or come up with lame excuses. He did not put off the task or try to wiggle his way out. He simply got the job done without asking how to get the job done. He used his resolve and work ethic and got the message to Garcia. People of this calibre are rare and are sought out by every nation, company, organization and family all over the world. They are extraordinary and precious, and we should all try to be like Rowan.

Why Aren't More People Like Rowan?

Perhaps, the reason why more people are not like Rowan is because many people have an entitlement mindset. As kids, their parents took care of them. As adults, their employer or the government replaced their parents. In other words, they feel that people, the company they work for, or the government owes them and will take care of them. When things get tough, instead of taking personal action they begin to point fingers of blame at someone or something. In some way, these people have not grown up. In order to be "The Guy", the entitlement mindset should be cast off and the personal philosophy of self-reliance ought to be adopted, once and forever. This level of maturity is essential to being "The Guy". Character is key and building a world-class level character is necessary for being awesome!

What Character Traits are Essential?

What then are some of the character traits that Rowan-like people have? These people, be they men or women, are people with a high sense of self-efficacy, that is, they believe in themselves and their abilities. They feel that if they fall short or simply fall, they will figure out a way. It is their natural way of thinking that obstacles are something to climb over or go around rather than something to be feared. These are people who fear very little in the first place. They persist. They have a high sense of duty. They have a high sense of pride in their personal results. They thrive on accomplishment and eagerly await their next challenge.

Here are the words of a retired Navy SEAL when asked: What lesson did you take in life as a result of your training? He said:

> *"If something is important to you,* ***never quit****. It's actually that simple; just decide that failure will not be because you quit. You may still fail, you might get fired, but not because you didn't try. What do they say, 'Showing up is half the battle'?"*

Anyone who desires to be like `Rowan should not despair; they should simply think to themselves: "If others can do it, so can I." If you feel this is something you would like to strive for, that is, being "The Guy", then go for it.

Change your reputation from whatever it is now. Just give it a concerted I-will-do-it-no-matter-what effort. And don't stop till you have done it!

A Real-Life Rowan (As narrated by Ahsan)

Allow me to share some details of someone I know who fits this description to a T. I have known this fellow for years. However, over the last ten years, after watching him just being himself, am I able to actually give you my testimony? It all started when I was moving from one house to another. I had bought a large TV cabinet that came unassembled. I recall putting that together when I first got it and it was awfully tedious and detailed; it took hours. So, when moving, I decided to leave the TV cabinet for the people who bought the house. I paid a lot of money for it, but felt it was impossible to take apart and reassemble since the instructions were long gone.

That is when my friend appeared on the scene. He looked at me strangely and said, "Why would you leave it? Leave it to me, I will take it apart and build it again at your new house". Honestly, I was thinking, "Really, do you know what you're getting yourself into?" Long story short, he asked for a screwdriver and next thing I knew, it appeared fully-assembled in my new house. You may think that this part of the story is pretty nifty, but there's more.

My friend knew of some other friends we have who needed some help with their small business. When he met with them, he asked them the details of their challenge and they explained all the hassles and obstacles they were facing. Again, he told them, "Is that it? Leave it to me". He worked diligently for them over several months and, to their amazement, solved their problems.

Another of his qualities is that he will show up to be a strong shoulder in a friend's hour of grief and loss. In fact, he will do this for people in general, not just friends he knows. He will just stand by to do whatever he can to ease the burden of the situation at hand, be that driving someone to the airport, picking up food, staying overnight at the hospital or being quietly present. He shows up first and leaves last, day after day, until the mourners return to their lives' routines. These are the things that I have seen with my own eyes and I am sure that this is really just the tip of the iceberg.

When I look at the things he has achieved in life so far, I am not surprised. He runs his own business, which he started from scratch ten years ago. His business is in a very competitive industry and yet is extremely successful. He married and has a wonderful family. As a person he is always cheerful and looks content. My friend, in my estimation, is a very determined person; he is not more privileged than others, he is not luckier, he just has a "get it done no matter what" mind set. Honestly, I hope that when I grow up, I can be just like my friend.

Whom do you know who can "carry a message to Garcia?" This quality of getting the job done and being reliable to the core is a quality that is not found in everybody. Those who have it share the same DNA of the brave and noble. A person who is reliable and has a high sense of pride in accomplishing a task deserves our respect. These are people whose actions do their talking. They become great individuals in their personal sphere and command admiration from all those around them. In times of difficulty, they are the first to offer help without being asked. When work needs to be done, they will be at the front of the line to begin work while others are still thinking about getting started, and will finish long after most people have already left for home. Such individuals, whom we can try to emulate, have a high sense of duty. They don't have an entitlement mentality; they are fiercely determined and have a "no matter what" mindset. Such people transmit character and excellence.

Action Items:

1. Identify someone you know who is "The Guy" or "The Girl".
2. Why do you think he or she is this way?
3. What character qualities does he or she have? Could you adopt those qualities too?
4. Take her for a coffee or lunch and ask her to explain her way of being.
5. If you are inclined, start being "The Guy" by getting things done when all others are making excuses.
6. Set up a challenge for yourself, where you lead a team or organize an event. Be bold and never grow old.
7. Think of the value and high regard you give to your friend and know that others will think the same of you if you are "The Guy".
8. What more can you achieve in life if you work on your character?
9. Make a list of five character traits you might like to work on over the next twelve months.

Chapter 5
Amazing Health

"Health is Wealth!"
Thomas Anonymous

"Health is not valued till sickness comes."
Thomas Fuller

"He who has health has hope; and he who has hope, has everything."
Thomas Carlyle

If ever there was a true statement, it would have to be that health is wealth. As said by Gerhardt Reimer, a Canadian farmer:

"A million dollars can't buy you one more day."

To be healthy is a true blessing and yet it eludes many people. What does it mean to be healthy and how do we achieve this? Let's define what health means. According to the World Health Organization, health is *"a state of complete physical, mental and social well-being and not merely the absence of disease or infirmity"*. You might also add spiritual well-being to the definition. We should consider this expanded definition of true health as the optimal state of existence to work towards. As you well know, health is earned by those who strive for it.

The following Islamic teachings present a good summary of how to look at the issue of overall health:

"O children of Adam! Look to your adornment at every time and place of worship, and eat and drink but exceed not the bounds; surely, He does not love those who exceed the bounds." Holy Qur'an (7:32)

"In the body is a piece of flesh, when it gets well, the whole body gets well and when it becomes unhealthy, the whole body gets unhealthy and hark! That piece is the heart."
Traditions by Bukhārī

Complete health has multiple parts that can be broken down into three main components—Physical, Mental and Spiritual. Let's look at each and discuss a strategy for optimal well-being that you can apply.

Physical Health

The first component to consider is the physical body, which is our vehicle for the rest of our lives. With proper care, we can try to make this wonderful mechanism last and function to its fullest potential. Our brain and our heart are the two most important organs that enable us to exist as we do. They define us. So how can we take care of these and the rest of our body? The formula is not complicated, and you intuitively know it. It's as simple as eating real food that is nutrient rich, rather than processed; eating to the point of comfortable fullness; and moving your body on a daily basis. More on that later.

What to Eat and Drink?

Consuming enough real protein and fats and getting most of the carbohydrates from vegetables and some fruit is a very sensible and healthy way to eat and live. Drinking mostly water at meal time and between meals is a simple way to maintain weight and stay hydrated. By following this routine, you can easily drink six to eight glasses of water a day. There's really no need for fruit juices, sports drinks and other sugary, calorie-laden drinks if you want to enjoy your best health. As for eating, a simple way to approach each meal is to divide your plate into three sections; half of your plate should contain a colourful array of vegetables, one quarter of your plate should have a palm-sized amount of meat or other protein, and the remaining quarter should have half to one cup of some sort of complex carbohydrate, such as rice, whole-grain bread or sweet potato. Add to that a bit of a healthy fat like nuts, avocado, butter, *ghee* or olive oil and you have a satiating meal that will easily carry you for hours.

The main objective of eating this way is to keep the body energized by consuming nutrients and keep blood sugar levels from spiking. By now, you probably have heard about the association between the consumption of sugar (or white bread, white pasta or white rice) which causes insulin release that affects blood sugar levels and results in the conversion of the remaining excess sugar into fat. If instead, you eat to keep your sugar (glycemic levels) moderate or low, you don't have insulin responding and you don't add to your fat stores. You can also avoid diabetes and arterial hardening, which are bad for your heart's health and possibly contribute to other serious conditions. The real enemy is excess sugar, not fat. Do some research on this to convince yourself. Go on a diet that drastically reduces sugar (read bread, rice and pasta) and increases nutrient-dense vegetables and fruit, lean sources of protein and small amounts of healthy fats, and see how you feel mentally and physically. You will probably drop a few pounds as a side effect. And of course, consult your doctor and get her okay before you proceed.

Look closely at all the modern advice about food and try to make sense of what is right for you to do. There are many fads and long-held beliefs that are being exposed as we speak. The so-called drink-one-glass-of-red-wine-a-day propaganda, for example, is unproven for heart health; in fact, it may precipitate heart disease, stroke and cancer. For non-drinkers, it is not worth the risk to your overall health which may be caused by even moderate amounts of alcohol. You will likely get more heart protection from eating an array of nutrient-filled fruits and vegetables and achieving better HDL cholesterol levels from daily exercise. To reduce added health risks in your life and gain the most benefit from nature, there's no need for alcohol in a life-long prescription for health. As the American Heart Association advises: If you don't drink alcohol, don't start! If you have made it a part of your life, try quitting for 30 days and see how much better you feel.

Junk Food is Designed to Be Irresistible

It is a curious fact that people did not worry about counting calories, fat content, sugar and salt levels, and ingredient lists until the past few decades. Natural and whole foods like nuts, eggs, rice, fruit, meat and vegetables don't require much calculating for nutrition content let alone unpronounceable ingredient lists. Now, we do worry and this is partly due to nutritional awareness and partly to confusion about what is "healthy" and what is not. The food of today is different from the food of yesterday. Food has become engineered to help bring more of it to a growing world population and preserved to keep it fresh for longer, as it is transported over long distances. Other changes have simply brought cheaper junk food and "food-like" substances to the masses, to generate profit for large corporations involved in food production, manufacturing or distribution—such as fast food restaurants and snack manufacturers. We now have "hyper-palatable foods" that on top of being processed have deliberate amounts of sugar, salt and fat to make you addicted—such as potato chips, cookies, ice cream, French fries and microwave popcorn. This type of food is making it hard for kids to enjoy the sweet taste of a crispy apple, because they would rather eat yummy fruit-flavoured cereal instead. It's difficult for taste buds to adjust to natural foods, when processed foods are lighting up pleasure centres of the brain.

Think about where your food comes from and how your body is meant to consume it. We can't live or thrive by eating artificial flavours and processed foods. These foods, if eaten in moderate to large quantities, cannot be healthy. Humans are omnivores not "processivores" which means we are meant to consume both plants and animals by design. We should respect this design by eating a variety of real, natural, unprocessed and chemical-free foods. Notice how junk foods leave you hungry again soon after eating, while natural foods fill you up and keep you full longer. There's the temptation of irresistible taste and flavour as well. Food scientists manipulate the taste of foods so that once you open up that bag of treats, you truly can't stop. For some, the first bite is the beginning of a food-trance high. Just be realistic—you know it's not real food, so eat it sparingly.

Don't Be SAD When Eating

With all this confusion and some deception happening in our food system, it's very difficult to decide what to do and how to eat—or is it? Does that tasty peanut butter really need heart-clogging hydrogenated oil, salt and sugar? Why not just eat natural peanut butter that has only one ingredient: ground peanuts? Have you observed that most people's grandmothers and their generation had much better health than people in their forties and fifties do today? Heart disease, diabetes, high blood pressure, cancer and chronic pain seems to be part of many people's lives today but they were not just two generations ago. As we started consuming the Standard American Diet or the SAD diet (yes, it is really ironic that the acronym spells 'SAD'), we see people getting sicker, fatter and generally ageing sooner than they did before. Sadly, this SAD approach to eating has reached the shores of countries around the world. Their once slimmer and healthier citizens are becoming fatter and sicker.

Go Back in Time for Diet Advice

It might be wise to ask people of our grandparents' generation what they ate growing up and do the same. From personal inquiry, we know that they ate mostly vegetables, lentils, beans, grains, butter, *ghee*, eggs, yoghurt, some fruit, very little meat—as it was expensive—and no processed junk food, because it did not exist for the most part. Also, meals were homemade and snacks consisted of nuts or fruit or homemade sweet dishes.

What if we started eating like those who lived in the early 1900s or earlier? What if our prepared food had just the minimum amount of ingredients and we could pronounce or recognize all of them? If we ate worry-free calories of primarily whole and natural foods, we could end the food confusion, ritualistic dieting, getting off track, making resolutions and repeating the whole cycle with nothing to show except marginal health. This is the path we should investigate and experiment with, for our physical well-being. Keeping things intuitive and simple is best, wouldn't you agree? From the Tradition of the Prophet Muhammad[pbuh], we learn:

> *"No human being has ever filled a container worse than his own stomach. The son of Adam needs no more than a few morsels of food to keep up his strength, doing so he should consider that a third of his stomach is for food, a third for drink and a third for breathing."*
> Ibn Maja[4]

---

4 A narrator of the Traditions of the Prophet Muhammad[pbuh].

Is Dr. Frankenstein Your Nutritionist?

Regardless of what eating philosophy you follow, one thing that is unanimous is that you should avoid processed foods. What does that leave us with? An opportunity to eat food that is as close to its original form as nature intended—food that is made of one ingredient only. Think eggs, honey, apples, lentils, spinach, chicken, fish or rice vs. foods that come in a box, bag or can. These foods are processed and mummified to last on the shelf for months and years. They will not digest in your system as easily as "pure and clean" foods and who knows how they are contributing to the main **"lifestyle diseases"** we see are reaching epidemic-like proportions (diabetes, cancer, heart disease). Why wait for some study or report to confirm what you already suspect?

Making a change away from eating "dangerous and dirty" is not easy, because you don't fall ill immediately. Many people don't believe these foods are harmful, because they don't get sick after eating "just one". Making a change in your eating habits is a challenge, but it can be done. Just remind yourself of what you want, which is health and energy vs. sickness and decreased energy. Then start gradually by replacing something like candy when the mood strikes for, say, blueberries. Your taste buds change over every 11 to 21 days. What that means is that you will gradually begin to notice what natural sweetness or natural saltiness is from foods and you will be able to resist the Dr. Frankenstein foods that might have been chasing you all your life. Within a month or two, you could make enough gradual changes in your diet to claim your healthiest and most energetic self ever! Do it for the benefits you will reap and the sickness you will avoid! You are on a health and longevity diet and are interested in feeling good to the end. You are not interested in declining in your forties, slipping further in your fifties, losing your vigour in your sixties and being fragile in your seventies.

How Important is Eating Right?

Consider the 80/20 rule for your overall health and well-being. This means that 80% of our health will come from the things we consume in the form of clean and nutrient-dense food and healthful drinks. The 20% that remains will be a direct result of how we stimulate our physical bodies through our normal routine, our exercise program and the rest we take each day. You can also interpret this as eating healthy 80% of the time and moving your body 20% of the time. Remember abs and healthy physiques are made in the kitchen, not the gym.

Don't Diet—Just Eat Well

One of the downsides to "dieting" is that it is not sustainable long term. If you must give up entire food groups or eat mainly one type of food, you will eventually quit. You might go strong for four to six days or weeks and then your resolve will fizzle. If you can, adopt a way of eating that you will do for life as a lifestyle, not as a crash diet. Your body can function on just about anything. However, what makes sense for you? What do you know is going to be easy to do long term? Some measure of regimentation will be necessary but start off with a realistic approach in the first place. You can't lose weight if you eat deep-fried food twice a week. You can't get plant-based nutrients if you don't eat vegetables. You can't feel clear-headed if you are crashing from a sugar high, be it from consuming vanilla cake or excessive amounts of rice. Also, be sure to eat enough; you can eat too little and guess what? You get "hungry". This is when hunger makes you angry. If you find yourself being snippy with your spouse, co-workers, friends and the cashier at the salad bar, eat a bit more. Let the weight come off slowly over time.

Get MAD Daily

Everyone has a great idea to promote health. Some say to eat certain foods. Others recommend herbal supplements and certain vitamins. The market is full of potions and drinks that promise youth in a bottle. The lure of these simple ideas are that they are easy to do. One idea to consider is to have a MAD salad each day. You could have it for lunch or for dinner. MAD stands for Massive Awesome Delicious. If you eat this type of salad, it will be a bit more involved than popping a pill or drinking a bottle of juice. Here is what goes in a MAD salad: first is the base, which can be any type of dark green leafy vegetable such as spinach or kale. Next is the bulk, which can be your favourite crunchy veggies like carrots, bell peppers, celery, tomatoes, radish, beets, cucumber etc. Finally, you need some protein-based toppings like grilled chicken or a handful of chickpeas or kidney beans and a tablespoon or two of chopped nuts like almonds, pecans, or walnuts. You can spritz a bit of lemon on top and a dash of salt and dusting of pepper or Cajun seasoning too. The effect on your health should be good, if not spectacular. Each day you are assured of getting ample nutrients, vitamins, minerals, protein, fibre and healthy fat. Over time, your cravings for junk food will fade and feeling good will be your lure for eating a MAD salad every day! Remember no one is stopping you from eating one for lunch *and* dinner.

Go Fast Once in a While

You have no doubt heard about fasting because it has been practiced for thousands of years by various people across all cultures and faiths. The Holy Qur'an states this fact in the verse below as a reminder,

"O ye who believe! Fasting is prescribed for you, as it was prescribed for those before you, so that you may guard against evil." Holy Qur'an (2:184)

Consider Intermittent Fasting or IF, as it is known today. All major religions have some kind of fasting ritual as part of their teachings and this can be a good practice whether you are religious or not. Why? To help with overall health maintenance you need to give the body a break from eating for most of the day to give the digestive system a rest. This can easily be done by those who are healthy and not in need of any regular medications or treatment. Fasting for a few days throughout the month can encourage more fat burning than we would normally experience when eating our normal meals on non-fasting days. The benefits are numerous: detoxing and cleansing the body, giving the internal organs a rest, promoting a sense of mental clarity, resetting your eating patterns and hunger levels, creating an awareness and sympathy of what hunger feels like for poor people, and even enjoying more restful sleep.

An example of a fasting model is the Muslim fast where no food or drink of any kind is consumed from sunrise to sunset. This practice is followed during the lunar month of Ramadhan which can be 29 or 30 days long. By observing fasting, we see many people renew themselves and undo damage done by eating the wrong things or by not living the right way outside of the month of Ramadhan. The observant Muslim also takes more time to reflect, study Islamic scriptures and live a more authentic Muslim way of life. This way, bad habits and wrong attitudes are shed by the end of this month along with some unneeded weight. This reflection and withdrawal from materialistic things is good for the mind as well as the soul and physical body. It's a complete reboot of the system that is better than any diet people can attempt. Another example of IF would be to skip breakfast and have your first meal of the day at lunch time. During your fasting hours, you will abstain from food but can drink water or your favourite hot beverage like tea or coffee without sugar. If you consider that dinner might end by 8 p.m. and you might have lunch at noon the following day, you will have fasted 16 hours. This could be practiced once or twice a week if you are so inclined. Why not give it a try? It might sound hard but until you try it, you will not know that it's easier than it sounds.

Move it or Lose it

Once you have your nutritional requirements sorted out, it is much easier to achieve overall health with a little regular exercise, which is the next step to overall health. Our bodies were designed to move. If you don't use it, your body will cramp and those aches will put you in a trap. That trap will be your body, which, due to its aches and pains, will prevent you from exercising. Your weight might then increase and further imprison you in your trap. All this could happen because you failed to go for a 30-minute walk every day. How awful would that be?

If you have not exercised in a very long time, you may like to start with a five to fifteen-minute walk daily. The concept of achieving 10,000 steps a day (about eight kilometres or five miles) might be a bit ambitious for a beginner. However, if a person were to do this as a lifelong habit, he would have strong legs, a strong heart, normal blood sugar levels, a trim waist, a clear mind, a sense of well-being, a positive self-image, unbreakable self-esteem and the admiration of his family—so starting with five minutes is not a bad bargain. Wouldn't it be great if at age 78, like Ahsan's Uncle Ashraf, you could skip 100 times and go for a two-mile walk and jog on a daily basis? Here is Uncle Ashraf's position on exercise: "When I was young,

I used to exercise five days a week; now that I am older, I exercise every day".

For a fit person, a combination of walking and sprinting, preferably in the outdoors, should be a goal for five days a week. For example, walk at a normal pace for two minutes and then speed up to jogging or sprinting speed to get to 75% of your maximum heart rate for one minute and then go back to normal speed for two minutes. Shift from normal to high gear and back to normal, three times without stopping and you will be able to achieve a good workout in just fifteen minutes versus jogging for an hour on a treadmill, which can injure your joints, not to mention bore you! Bonus points to those who are near a beach or a large field where they can do the walk/sprint workout on a soft surface instead of a concrete sidewalk.

Be Like Arnold!

Another consideration is strength training with your own body weight or dumbbells. Rather than work out for one hour or more in a gym, you could focus on a 15-20 minute routine that aims to create strength and toning, as your training goal. To make your muscles respond and to be effective, you don't need to annihilate them with heavy weights or super sets; you simply need to stimulate them with core moves and do your strength training routine two to three times a week with at least one day's rest in between. This should also give you good muscle tone and time for recovery between sessions. Your strength training should include push-ups, squats, calf raises, triceps presses, shoulder presses, bicep curls and pull-ups or chin-ups. Combining these simple exercises in one short workout can stimulate your muscles in very little time. Aim for ten repetitions of each exercise and don't worry if you can't do ten of everything just yet. You will progressively work up to ten as you increase your strength over a few weeks of trying each exercise. It's more important to focus on good form than hammering out repetitions quickly.

Once you feel comfortable doing these workouts for a few weeks, add a few more exercises like planks and bicycle crunches to the routine and you have a complete workout with all the exercises you need for a total body workout—no health magazine, poster or special DVD required. For example, try to do twenty bicycle crunches to work your core muscles—remember, you can't spot reduce fat to get those abs, but you can still strengthen your core by working your midsection. Next, try to hold the plank position for at least twenty seconds and then work up to holding this position for one minute and you will develop overall core strength with no gym membership and no money wasted on gadgets and exercises that don't work. An effective exercise regimen will include both cardio and strength training. If you are super keen and motivated to look and feel your best, you would do strength training at least twice a week; cardio four times a week and do no exercise one day a week. Simple, really.

The Fountain of Youth

According to one physiotherapist, the body was designed to last forty years. Yikes! What does he mean by that? From practical experience, many over forty-year-olds will attest that at this age, their joint and muscle pains began in full force. The major client base for massage therapists, chiropractors, osteopaths and physiotherapists is the age forty-plus crowd. To combat your body's tendency to get sore and achy, consider incorporating a daily routine of stretching your body, as in the yoga tradition. Have you noticed how all the tight and sore muscles are on the back of your body? When people complain about sore muscles it usually is to do with their upper or lower back, hamstrings, calves, shoulders or neck. This is due to the fact that most of the day we are hunched forward in a sitting position. In so doing, over time our muscles get sore because they are shortening and getting tight. To resolve this, we need to stretch in the opposite direction and thereby lengthen and reset those muscles. If you can't picture this, you can look up stretches for the back, neck and shoulders that will involve positions like the Superman, the cat, the cobra, the lotus, the pigeon, various calf and hamstring stretches, and the use of a foam roller for your upper and lower body.

You may also be surprised to know that sore knees and glutes have little to do with the site of the pain and more to do with supporting muscles like the quadriceps and psoas muscles respectively. Lower back pain, which is the biggest complaint that most people have, can often be aggravated by tight glutes! The idea is to keep your muscles loose and prevent them from shortening and freezing up. Doing stretches on a daily basis is absolutely a must; it's like adding oil to your creaky joints, as if you were the Tin Man in *The Wizard of Oz*. Get a yoga video, book or join a class to learn the stretches and the proper technique to avoid injury. Always do stretches that are gentle and within your comfort zone. If you go to a yoga class and the instructor encourages you to stand on your head, don't do it; you risk seriously hurting your spine or delicate disks. You don't have to do pretzel stretches to benefit from stretching.

Ease into Your Exercise Routine

The best reason to walk rather than run long distances is the lower chance of injury associated with walking, which means it is something you can keep doing on a regular basis. The purpose of exercise is to develop strength and avoid injuries. Ironically, a lot of people push themselves so hard at the start with heavy weight training or long distance running that they end up either pulling a muscle, or damaging their joints very badly. This makes them unable to train for many days or weeks at a time, which defeats the purpose of achieving and maintaining optimal health. If you become a runner and end up with knee surgery, what is the point?

Try to train your body in such a way that you are able to move in a youthful way. Many people in their fifties, let alone forties, are unable to hop over a puddle or jump sideways to avoid a soccer ball headed their way. If you are able to squat and stand back up without losing your balance, you are young no matter what your age. Likewise, if you can pick up a basketball that is rolling on the ground and pass it or shoot it twenty feet away, you are fit, nimble and really living.

Before you start any routine, take measurements of your hip, waist, chest, shoulders and arms. Next, book a physical check-up at your doctor's office and get her approval to proceed. This advice is not to be discounted. Regardless of your age or physical condition, make sure your doctor says you are healthy enough to exercise.

Sleep Well and Excel

As Benjamin Franklin stated:

"Early to bed and early to rise, makes a man healthy, wealthy and wise."

Once eating and general exercise is tackled, the topic of rest must be discussed if you want to have a complete picture of health. You can eat well and have a toned body but if you go one or two nights with disturbed sleep or not enough sleep, you feel less than 100%. You need sleep to feel your best. Various studies discuss how much we need to sleep. Some say that we should get a minimum of six hours of sleep each night while others say it should be eight hours or more. The bottom line is to get a deep and restful sleep every night and this starts with good preparation before bedtime. First, your room should be dark and quiet. Make sure you have dark curtains, no electronic lights flashing from clocks or other devices, and consider wearing an eye mask. Also, find a pillow that supports your head and neck so you don't toss and turn. Often, people are tired because their pillow is malfunctioning all night.

You should not sleep with an active or anxious mind. So, if something is on your mind, write it down somewhere to get it out of your head. Better yet, resolve knotty issues a few hours before sleeping so you are not thinking about what needs to be done or endlessly repeating problems in your head. Eating and drinking should likewise stop several hours before you sleep. This will promote a deeper sleep, too. Consider avoiding things that will stimulate the mind before you nod off, like TV and the computer. Take a break from all bright lights and sounds an hour before you lie down. You can do this by turning down the lights and noise around you so that you will be preparing yourself for sleep. You may like to recite a prayer or two before you fall asleep and ask God for a restful sleep and to awaken fresh in the morning. We all remember mornings where we felt truly rested and energized by our sleep. This state has to be earned by making conscious efforts, not just flopping on your bed and hoping you feel good in the morning.

What to Do if You Lost Your Mojo?

A lot of people complain that they are tired all day long even after a full night's sleep. While there could be some medical condition that is present, there are a few things to do before you give up and accept defeat. Be honest with yourself and ask if you are eating well. Also, are you exercising? And, are you getting enough sleep? If any of these three components are off or absent, should you be surprised at your failing energy levels? Having all-day energy is awesome. Ideally, you should feel refreshed when you wake up and have ample energy to last a whole day. When it is bed time, only then should you feel "tired".

Friends: How Many of Us Have Them?

How many friends do you have? Do you meet people on a daily basis? Do you feel connected to others? We as humans are social beings and we were meant to live in groups, not in isolation. One of the most unfortunate situations is that of people dying of loneliness; often these people are neglected seniors or parents. The healthiest people are those that have a strong link with other people. They have good social networks made up of real people with whom they meet regularly and who contribute to their general well-being. We should all have a social network of friends and family and reconnect with those from whom we may have become detached. This does not mean your 500 or more Facebook friends. We're talking about the five to ten people you spend most of your time with because you have a positive connection with them and they have positive effect on you.

You also have the opportunity to make new friends every day through your daily interactions and chance meetings with people. Although you may have good old friends, be ready to make new friends because some of the people you grew up with will move away; others may grow apart and some are only fair-weather friends. Finding a true friend is not easy, so if you do have one or more, cherish them!

Be Connected and Make Connections

One of the greatest acts of charity is a smile to a passer-by and this in a small way counts as a social connection. Even better, get out there and start a real conversation.

Attending community events and social gatherings also helps you to be a member of the human tribe, so participate and help everyone improve his or her social network one connection at a time. Join a club, get out and volunteer, play with kids, throw a party for someone just because he helped shovel snow off your driveway. Enjoy the ensuing conversations, laughter and celebrations! Remember, when you meet people, you get out of your own head and can see how your life compares to those with whom you are interacting. This might give you some added perspective on how to appreciate the things that are going well and not so well in your own life.

Faith Does a Body Good

No discussion on overall health would be complete without mentioning the spiritual connection to health. This has the added benefits of giving you a community to which you belong, an opportunity to demonstrate faith through actions and also, peace of mind. Be a part of your church, synagogue, mosque, gurdwara, or temple. When you are shoulder to shoulder with others in such a setting, you will find a certain peace and sense that you are not alone. Being connected with something that is greater than yourself and reflecting on life, and the purpose of creation can give you comfort.

The Holy Qur'an eloquently points out:

"And when My servants ask thee about Me, say: 'I am near. I answer the prayer of the supplicant when he prays to Me. So they should hearken to Me and believe in Me, that they may follow the right way." (2:187)

And again:

"O ye who believe! Seek help with patience and prayer; surely, Allah is with the steadfast."
(2:154)

Clearly there is power in prayer or worship so we should take advantage of its benefits however we may pray and whatever faith we belong to.

According to the Traditions of the Prophet Muhammad[pbuh], he is reported to have said:

"Verily there is cure in Prayer."

According to a Muslim scholar, as reported in a monthly Urdu magazine, *Tahazibul Akhlaq*, of Aligarh, India, a Muslim who offers Prayers regularly may have less chance of getting painful arthritis since they are exercising their bones and joints regularly through Prayers—the physical act of worship in Islam. How many people today suffer from various kinds of pain due to inactivity, poor circulation and feelings of depression? Sometimes the answer to all of this is right in front of us in the form of daily prayers which can at least help us reduce pain and suffering by combining physical, mental and spiritual components together in a beneficial way.

Believing that there is a God who is always available to hear us and answer our prayers offers hope and direction in life. As the Irish proverb reminds us:

"When you go to sleep, give your problems to God; He will be up all night anyway!"

Our emotional health and our overall well-being depend mainly on having a solid spiritual core. Combined with physical training and proper sleep, faith can inspire, educate, motivate and create new ways to not just survive but also thrive in life. Give your whole being a spiritual workout each day so you cannot just avoid sickness, but achieve optimal health for your whole life!

Putting it all Together

Let's say a young man named Abraham wants to feel healthy. After considering the ideas in this chapter, he would make sure that he eats natural foods at least six days a week. Additionally, he would make his meals at home and avoid any sugary drinks or fast food. Abraham would also go out for brisk walks of at least 30 minutes every day. To nurture his spirit, he would observe prayers daily. In addition, Abraham would sleep for eight hours every day so that he wakes up naturally and feels refreshed. Keeping to the 80/20 rule, Abraham allows himself one day each week to skip exercising or being strict with his diet. As a result, Abraham has maintained good overall health while being less than perfect. After following this routine, Abraham felt so well that he decided to keep going and make this his new lifestyle. He has also managed to get through difficult situations in life with more focus and less stress than in the past, when he didn't have any particular routine or structure.

A Cornucopia of Healthy Tips

Here is a random list of ideas in no particular order of importance:

1. Cut up some veggies, ginger, and garlic on the day you buy them and keep them in containers ready to toss into your morning omelette; MAD salad or dinner stir-fry. You will avoid the mental block of food prep if you spend thirty minutes chopping things in advance with a dicer or mandolin. This should provide three to four days' worth of chopping.

2. Eat from a smaller dinner plate or buy a plate that is portioned in three parts. This way you can fill the big portion with veggies and the two smaller parts with a protein such as meat or lentils and a complex carbohydrate such as rice or sweet potatoes.
3. Drink water throughout the day to keep your system flushed. Keep your body hydrated and don't wait for signs of thirst! If your urine is dark yellow, up your water intake.
4. Eat slowly; you will feel full and satiated after eating your meal. They say it takes twenty to thirty minutes for your brain to receive the signal from your stomach that you are full.
5. Chew your food seventy times. Most people chew five or six times and swallow large chunks of food. By chewing a high number of times so that you virtually liquefy your morsels, you will achieve ease of digestion and better nutrient absorption, and you will naturally eat more slowly!
6. When you first wake up, before you take that first drink of water, take a sip of water and swish it in your mouth like mouthwash and spit it out. After this take another sip and gargle two or three times and spit out all the "cooties" that settled in your throat overnight. Now, drink your first glass of water for the day. You will effectively be cleaning out your throat area where bacteria hang out and may find that you don't get sick with colds and flu as often.
7. Wash your hands with soap and water throughout the day and don't touch your eyes, nose or mouth with unclean hands so as to avoid cold and flu germs.
8. Eat fruit for dessert.

9. Take a good multi-vitamin every day.
10. Don't drive distracted. Don't text or read texts. Don't take calls. You are more valuable than the call coming in.
11. Avoid eating too much salt. One idea is to not have a salt shaker on your table. Remember, salt is added to many processed foods.
12. Floss your teeth daily; it's good for your heart and your breath.
13. Make a green smoothie every day. All you need is a powerful blender, frozen fruit for sweetness, one cup of water, a scoop of vanilla whey protein, a handful of spinach or kale or greens powder, and a tablespoon of nuts. It tastes like a guilty pleasure and you get your "vitameatavegimins".
14. Buy some whole and natural psyllium husk. Add a teaspoon to your smoothie or drink it plain in an eight-ounce glass of water to add bulk to your diet and keep things moving.
15. Make exercise the same kind of habit as brushing your teeth, one that is non-negotiable!
16. Try exercise DVDs for days that are too hot or cold to go outdoors.
17. Try Nordic pole walking. This is what cross-country ski folks in Europe started doing in the off-season. Today, especially in Germany and Norway, people use this form of walking with ski poles as the more highly evolved method of walking. When you walk you engage your leg muscles; when you use the poles, your arms, forearms, shoulders and back engage and you achieve a total body workout.
18. Try rebounding on a mini-trampoline (the better ones have bungee cords rather than springs). This will give you a great cardio workout, make

your core solid, improve your leg strength, condition your hip muscles, relieve pain in your knees, strengthen your feet and promote circulation of your lymphatic system. It's also a great way to connect with your inner child. Remember how fun it was to jump on your bed?

19. Do squats to avoid hip soreness and knee pain. You should do them daily, twenty to fifty times. Learn how to do them properly so that you don't stress or injure your knees. You can do "air-squats" without holding dumbbells or do them with dumbbells.
20. Get a foam roller and roll out muscle soreness in your back and legs. You can also lie on it to stretch the small of your back after a long day of sitting.
21. Get up from your seat and move for five to ten minutes per hour of sitting. Many people have a sedentary job, plus they drive everywhere and sit at home in front of the TV. Their daily sitting time exceeds what nature intended. Keep your body active throughout the day so your body and its various systems stay vital and engaged. Use it or lose it.
22. Try to keep your posture nice and proper. That means walk tall with your head and ears aligned above your shoulders. Poor posture makes you look old and is a habit that can be changed. You will feel alert and generally more positive too!
23. Keep a daily Exercise and Food Journal. Buy a black hard-cover note book and record what exercise you did that day and what food and snacks you ate. Don't dismiss this as too much work. Just do it for 90 days and see how it guides your actions.
24. Be happy. Guard your mind from stress, anxiety

and the blues! If you are feeling positive because you are thinking positive, you are less likely to give up on your total health lifestyle.

25. If you are having a meeting with a colleague, why not go together for a walk and discuss business? If you always did this, you will beat the danger of sitting all day long.
26. Go on a walk with your mother. You will both be healthier and can spend some quality time together too.
27. On Sunday morning, instead of sleeping in, why not wake up early, go on a one-hour family hike and come back and effortlessly make everyone healthy veggie omelettes using the veggies you already cut up on Friday?
28. When eating your dinner, start by eating a MAD salad or MAD soup and then move on to the healthy main course. You will feel relaxed knowing you are full—full of nutrients and not excess calories.
29. Keep a scale and weigh yourself once a week in the morning before you eat breakfast. The best kind is the model you find in a doctor's office; you can buy one for the house if you are truly the serious type. This way you will be able to spot creeping pounds before they become a problem. If you are trying to lose weight, weigh yourself at most once a week because on some days, water retention will add pounds to the scale and can potentially dishearten you from staying with your healthy routine.
30. Next time you go to meet with friends at a restaurant or at their home for dinner, eat a small healthy meal before you go. This way you won't be ravenous and you will be able to eat clean. They might also be impressed by your

constant discipline (we won't tell them your secret).

31. Don't be a carbotarian, that is, someone who eats excessive bread, *roti*, *naan*, tortillas, pasta, and rice. A half cup or one cup of rice or pasta should be the upper limit at any one sitting. One slice of toast or an open-face sandwich is better for your belly measurement than eating two. If you are lucky enough to have hot fresh *roti* or tortillas come off the stove as you are eating, limit yourself to just the one and ask for a small one, too. Instead, fill up on veggies and just control yourself.
32. Never get too hungry because once you do, your willpower will go down the tubes!
33. Get your blood work done so you know if you have low HDL and high triglycerides (this is not good). Know what your blood sugar levels are (remember the only way off dialysis is transplant or death); know what your blood pressure is (it's called the silent killer because you can't feel it).
34. Keep your belly flat because visceral fat is not your friend.

Don't be fanatical; it's okay to have a break from all this advice but a break is to be brief, occasional and not an excuse to go back to your old habits. If you are serious about health, remember that you cannot go back to your old ways!

If you understand the laws of nature, you can use them to your advantage. No one will stop you from studying and implementing these ideas. Give yourself the gift of good health and take responsibility for it. This is a choice and not a chance. You can have vibrant health in every sense of the word. And remember:

"Doing something consistently is 100 times better than doing something occasionally."
Ahsan and Shazad

Action Steps

1. Take stock of all food in your house and remove processed food along with any cookies, candies and sweet drinks such as colas, fruit juices, sports drinks and meal replacements. Also get rid of anything low fat, sugar free or anything remaining that has 'diet' in its name. What's left should be an almost empty fridge and pantry allowing you to shop for vegetables, fruit, rice, whole-grain bread, lentils, herbs, spices, eggs, butter, *ghee*, yoghurt, coconut oil, nuts, chicken, fish and lamb or beef, all examples of real food.

2. Make food at home at least five days a week using your new ingredients and make more than you can eat so you have enough for healthy leftovers the next day. You can grill, sauté, bake or roast your ingredients and season with herbs and spices instead of adding salt. Try replacing refined table salt with sea salt and use less.

3. Avoid all sugary drinks and juices for at least 21 days while you are eating healthy. Snack on unsalted nuts and raw vegetables only if you are truly hungry. For one or two days in a week, try avoiding eating for as long as you can after you wake up, so that your first meal is lunch after noon and then eat a normal lunch and dinner meal rather than trying to force yourself to have three meals that day. Once or twice a week you

can have a planned cheat meal allowing you to eat a reasonable portion of whatever you feel like having without guilt (note how you feel a few hours after eating this way). You may find yourself less motivated to have these over time, since you prefer the way healthy eating makes you feel.

4. Make two lists and compare them. The first list contains all the reasons you want to be healthy. The second list contains all the excuses you have for not being healthy. Let the lists motivate you. Put the lists on your bathroom mirror and read them while flossing.

5. Whatever your religious tradition may be, consider offering your daily prayers. Also, consider going to congregational Prayers at least once a week and pray with others. If you have other beliefs, you could make a habit to give thanks each day for all that you have using some kind of gratitude exercise. Those who believe in God might like to ask for His help to face the challenges life presents, while you are also doing your part to help make things better.

6. Work while standing for a few minutes each hour if you normally sit all day at your job. For example, try standing up for phone calls and get up every 45 minutes to take a short walk around your office before returning to your chair. You can benefit more quickly from your exercise efforts if you make sure that you don't stay sitting for long periods of time. Doing so can improve your productivity, focus and creativity throughout the day and also helps you stretch

out so you are less likely to have cramps, joint pain and repetitive stress injuries.

7. Start tracking your physical activity. There are plenty of apps and gizmos to use. If you are old school and like simple but effective methods, simply take a paper calendar and mark it with a check mark each day you exercised. At the end of the month, if you checked 24 days, you just got a grade of 80% or an 'A'. Use gold star stickers (why not?) and aim for consistency.

8. Be social. Meet your friends. Make new friends. Put something in to your schedule like going out for coffee with your buddy or reading to children at the library.

Chapter 6
Equanimity

"The Lord's favours cannot be forced out of His hand; some even while awake attain them not; on others He confers these, shaking them awake."
Adi Granth[5], Sri Raga Mahalla 4 M. 1.

"Great thoughts reduced to practice become great acts."
Ali bin Abu Talib, the Fourth Caliph of Islam

"It is what it is. You can only control your response to conditions around you, not the conditions."
Ahsan and Shazad

Equanimity: What does this mean?

When life is going smoothly, it's easy to have a calm and cheery outlook. In fact, the smallest bit of good news sets our mood on a high level. But when things go off track, many people lose their composure and some might take days to get back on the course of feeling "even" again. Would it not be nice to be unfazed by "things" that happen to you? Have we not wasted hours or even days being upset about something that today we can barely remember? Who suffered needlessly? Staying "even of mind" is the basic definition of the word equanimity. It is also having the quality of calmness and composure regardless of conditions

[5] The Adi Granth—or as it is presently called, Guru Granth—is a voluminous text that is the main Scripture of Sikhism. It includes hymns that describe the qualities of God and the purpose of meditation on God's name. Essentially based on the compositions of Baba Guru Nanak, it also includes some contributions by later Gurus.

in life. Possessing a permanent sense of equanimity is something we can try to cultivate if we make it a way of being rather than an evanescent state. When life is not going according to plan and you are able to say to yourself that regardless of this setback, annoyance, challenge or tragedy, "I will be calm and cheerful", you can claim to be a victor over yourself. Most of us find it hard to be that "evolved", but we could be, if we tried. This will require making the quality of equanimity a priority. You need to literally keep reminding yourself on a daily basis that being accepting of things and circumstances is better than being affected by things and circumstances. Acting and not reacting is the basic strategy.

Even Mind

We live in a world of hopes, dreams and uncertainty. Avoiding uncertainty is not possible; what is possible is composing yourself so that you remain calm, cool, and collected should difficulty befall you. You can try to take a philosophical approach to remain unattached and disconnected from the world (not easy to do and perhaps impractical), you could turn to harmful intoxicants as many people do (self-medication is often deadly) or you can train yourself to be resilient and strong of mind. An end in itself is having an even mind. This is the state of mind to which all people in all times have aspired; however, this proves to be an elusive state that few people learn to cultivate.

There are some people who are not fazed by anything. There is the case of a saintly person who lived in India in the late 1800s who had written many books. Once his young son got hold of some matches and burned a nearly completed manuscript to ashes. Instead of losing his cool or being understandably distressed, he calmly resolved to re-write the book all over again. The same person was embroiled in two separate court cases against him that would have either resulted in heavy fines or possibly, the death penalty. It is reported that when you met him, you would not ever know that he was in the midst of such pressure. He was calm and cheerful; carrying on as though nothing was going on. In the end, he was exonerated on both counts; the most serious being an accusation of murder.

So what about the rest of us? The good news is that like anything that involves the mind and control of it, it is not impossible! Having an even mind is an achievable way of being, if one practices ways to reach that state. At the heart of the matter is control of one's thoughts and resulting emotional state. If thoughts produce feelings, one has only to focus on one or the other to produce a desired emotional state. You can focus your thoughts to be directed away from that which concerns you and towards something that gives you joy, or you can focus on feeling joyful and grateful. Perhaps having equanimity is really about reconnecting to joy. To be joyful is our natural state. Take a look at any child. They are always happy. They play. They find joy in the simplest of things, like squishing peas between their fingers or chasing butterflies in the back yard or hugging their teddy bears. Perhaps we leave joy behind in childhood and become too serious as we grow up. We stop squishing peas between our fingers!

Suggestions for Achieving an Even Mind

For many, the surest method of achievement begins with remembrance of God and knowing that He is a living God with whom you can have a direct relationship. A lot of people perform their religious duties and prayers where they supplicate to the Supreme Being that is "there but distant", rather than calling on God as a friend who is near and personal. By making direct supplications, you begin to develop a personal relationship with your Creator. As such, you accept that you may not know what the future holds but that you know who holds the future. You resign yourself to and trust God's decree.

As with all goal achievement, there has to be a deliberate focus on the end state (equanimity) in order for it to be yours to keep. If you reach a stage where you are always in a state of "even mind" you should give yourself a pat on the back. This is not necessarily easy. One's thoughts and interpretations about what happens in life will have to be tuned up and checked continuously. People who face change in life with an attitude of acceptance do much better than those who wallow in the "why me" frame of mind. Life, like it or not, will change on you so don't be surprised when it does. Also, don't become disheartened. Checking in with one's feelings and thoughts throughout the day will also be helpful. If you feel off track, you will need to pull out a few rabbits from your hat to bring you back on track.

One such rabbit to enhance this equanimity mind set is with regular physical exercise. As mentioned earlier, without a doubt, daily exercise is important to your mental outlook as much as it is for your physical well-being. To relax the mile-a-minute mind, one needs to relax the body.

One can also set aside the first five minutes of each day on inward reflection. Rather than jumping out of bed in a hurry, sit on the edge of your bed and collect your thoughts by focusing the mind on a single helpful and uplifting thought, especially gratitude for the bounties bestowed on you, or recalling a feeling of joy such as hugging your kid or parent, hitting a perfect golf shot or reliving a beautiful sunset. Some call this meditation and others call this mindfulness. It needs to be practiced as a skill and habit and will promote relaxation of the mind. **Mind your mind!**

Another tactic is eating food that promotes a relaxed body. Eat food that is full of nutrients so your body can function at optimum. Moreover, watch your stimulants; reduce your caffeine and sugar intake. All these suggestions—prayer, exercise, mindful reflection and diet—should be done daily! If you were to do this occasionally, you would not get the healing and restorative benefits of this "method". This requires 100% commitment and effort.

The benefits of adopting this approach of overarching equanimity are too valuable to ignore: feeling calm, responding gracefully to life's curveballs and fastballs. Perhaps, most importantly, you will be effective as a person and pleasant to be with for your spouse, children, friends, co-workers and even strangers. They will pick up on your calmness. You may start to *not* dwell on things. Perhaps you will be the sort of person who really pays attention to people and holds their gaze as you speak to them. Indeed, you will start enjoying the moments of your life, rather than looking back and not remembering important days and events, letting life become a massive blur. Be joyful; be even of mind.

What is Holding You Back?

What does your life look like? What does your life feel like? The only person that can answer the first question would be someone who knows you and can observe your life. The second question can only be answered by you. The issue is that observing yourself is not all that easy or intuitive. Self-examination is not easy, because you are the actor in your own "movie" and it's hard to be a member of the audience and observe. Although it may be hard and awkward, it is not impossible.

If you try to be a member of the audience, you will undoubtedly come to realize that we are all experiencing our lives based on how we view the world. How we view the world in turn is shaped by our personal values and beliefs that are ingrained in our minds from the time we were children. Arguably, these personal values and beliefs, were implanted in our minds from our parents, our school teachers, even our friends, and the media and society. These inherited values and beliefs become fused as our visual lens by which we ultimately experience life events. In other words, how you were influenced (read moulded and shaped by others), influences how you experience life. The cool thing is that you are not stuck being the current version of you. If something contributing to who you are is not serving you well, get rid of it! Give yourself permission to take over from here.

What if a person awakens to this universal situation that we all face? What if she becomes not only a member of the audience, but takes on the role of director? Could she not re-define who she is and create new futures for herself that are more exciting and colossal than ever imagined or settled for? She can literally "direct" her enjoyment of life by seeing herself as someone who is not a statue (carved in stone), but rather a diamond in the rough, who will emerge with facets of possibilities and brilliance of potential.

Bounce Back Bigger and Better

No doubt, it's easier said than done. Sometimes, people are being held back by a belief or a negative life event or experience. People have a variety of negative experiences in life. Some people bounce back from adversity while others don't. The key to bouncing back is having an empowering outlook on life. For example, trivial things make some people upset—not just upset, but deeply distressed. For others, a genuine trauma is taken in stride. Even with childhood-imprinted events, some people get over it while others stay trapped as victims. Let's take a look at someone who lost his job. He could feel like he was the victim of the situation and be shattered or he could view it differently. That view might include the fact that his company made a decision to let a few hundred employees go to stay viable and that he was just one of them. That would be a mature way to look at it. In essence, he could understand that he was not specifically targeted by the company or by divine destiny; rather, he was part of an overall economic reality. This view would be more empowering and cause him to actively look for a new opportunity rather than wallow in a pity party for weeks, months or—years!

Sometimes, a calamity becomes a defining event in a positive way. A calamity can be a blessing because once you bravely face it, you build your character. All great men and women in history were shaped by facing adversity, often adversity that appeared early in their lives. It's like the old saying: when the going gets tough; the tough get going! Strengths appear that they did not know they had. An interesting fact is that whether or not you are a believer in God, the opportunity to emerge victorious is available to you. If you are a believer, it may be easier because you will no doubt include prayer as part of your strategy to overcome your hardship. Once you pray, you believe things will get better. You also feel much better. In our mind, if God is on our side, everything will be okay. You are beseeching the most powerful Being in the universe and you begin to relax, often instantly. Even if the solution to your problem does not present itself quickly, you feel encouraged that you will be able to face all challenges until your problem subsides.

So, to overcome the problems of life, be they large or small, we need to remember that God does not punish good people. Bad things happen to good people, but they are not from God. Ninety-nine percent of tragedy is not directed at you. These things just happen. If we analyze the problem, we may realize the problem was caused by our own doing or else that we were part of a widespread phenomenon or event as described just above. A soldier who goes to war knows that he can be shot and killed. The more time he spends in the front lines of battle, the greater the chance he will be shot. So, going back to the example of the person who lost their job, he would say to himself, "People lose their jobs every day. I will try to find a new job and when I do, I will not sit in fear that I might lose that job too. Instead of trying to avoid the job loss tragedy, I will deal with it if it happens again."

Often, our level of faith will determine how easy the acceptance of the problem will be. Psychologists find people of faith fare better and women in particular even more so as their faith is stronger than that of men. But what about those people who worry about what's around the corner?

These are thankfully a small breed of people whom we might call "worrywarts". These folks worry out of habit. If a big worry does not take hold of their thoughts, there are plenty of small worries that occupy their thoughts. The best advice to these folks as mentioned elsewhere is to not worry in advance. Deal with your problems if and when they happen. Don't pay the price of worry in advance. True, you may be hit with a calamity or disaster, but there is no need to worry in advance. We will go into more detail on worry elimination in the next chapter.

Accept, Affirm, Have Faith

To achieve a supreme state of resolve, calmness of mind and composure, try not to focus solely on your challenges. Focus instead on your abilities and your faith in yourself. Should you feel inclined, pray for increase on both counts. **Accept** your situation; **Affirm** your belief in yourself to handle the situation; and, have **Faith** that all will work out. Things tend to work out in the end, don't they? Resolve to be in a state of equanimity, which essentially means being accepting of what life throws at you with a brave attitude and remaining steadfast! As the

Roman Emperor Marcus Aurelius (121-180 C.E.) wrote in his famous Meditations:

> *"When force of circumstance upsets your equanimity, lose no time in recovering your self control, and do not remain out of tune longer than you can help. Habitual recurrence to the harmony will increase your mastery of it."*

Action Steps

1. How do you react when things don't go your way? Do you take it in stride or freak out?
2. What ideas will you use to become more "even of mind"?
3. Schedule time in your day to check in with your feelings.
4. Give up some of your sweets.
5. Give up one extra cup of coffee or *chai*.
6. Get moving!
7. Make a list of things that set you off and face them head on!
8. Spend time with a friend who really knows you. Together, try to figure out why you are the way you are. Are there behaviours that hold you back? Can you rewrite your movie?
9. Make a list of challenges in life that you faced and from which you came back stronger. This list will put you in a positive mood and remind you of your skills and resources!
10. Talk to someone you know who has gone through a few tough times in life and ask them how they managed those situations.

Chapter 7
Kicking the Worry Habit

"Do not be anxious about anything, but in everything by prayer and supplication with thanksgiving let your requests be made known to God."
Philippians 4:6

"A man who suffers before it is necessary, suffers more than is necessary."
Lucius Annaeus Seneca

"I believe God is managing affairs and that He doesn't need any advice from me. With God in charge, I believe everything will work out for the best in the end. So what is there to worry about."
Henry Ford

Monsters Under Our Bed and Inside Our Head

In our minds, there seems to be a natural response mechanism sometimes referred to as the fight or flight response. It was extremely helpful in the old days when we lived in a hunt-or-be-hunted age. When we worry over something or feel anxious, the mind causes the body to either become tense and ready to fight the perceived threat or to run to safety (flight). The heart may start beating faster, muscles may tense, your hands may sweat or your stomach feels as if it is in knots. Oddly, the body will have such a response even if you imagine a threat. There might not be a monster in your closet, but the thought of it will bring this feeling on. How do we beat the monsters? Can we do this once and for all? Can you simply command yourself to worry about what you can control?

An understanding that fear or worrisome thoughts are

really "What-If" scenarios playing in your mind is essential to beating this forever. These What-If thoughts cause real distress. We can't live in a What-If world. This debilitating thought is best combated by the following thought: Come what may, I will be OK! I will figure it out. I am a smart and rational person. This thought takes you from a mental state of helplessness to a state of power and control. The more you let the dominating thought go, the less the thought will dominate you. The real trick is to get rid of the What-If thinking which is the culprit of causing the physical and mental discomfort. If anything, you ought to think what if something good happens? Be the most optimistic person you know! You need to be ready to face problems with the mindset that you can handle any sized problem, because you are stronger than the problem! At the end of the day you have to face your fears and phobias. Never back away from them. Expose yourself to them and slay the dragon once and for all. It also does not hurt to know that you have God (your source of strength) on your side, so remind yourself of this. As Nelson Mandela encouraged us:

> *"I learned that courage was not the absence of fear, but the triumph over it. The brave man is not he who does not feel afraid, but he who conquers that fear."*

You've got to have courage, my love!

The Cost of Worry

Maybe one can argue that a small bit of concern is not a bad thing but we all know that full-out worry is a high cost to pay. People may miss out on many opportunities because of worry if it gets out of hand. Take for example the person who avoids going to certain places, because they worry about something bad happening on the way or when they get there. This person may not see their friends or relatives often or miss out on promotions at work. Perhaps we need more perspective and practice to overthrow this distorted thought. We can also try to take the advice from the Bhagavad Gita:

> *"Abandon all attachment to the results of action and attain supreme peace."*

Let's make a decision not to pay the high cost of worry. Your health can suffer, your social life can be affected and your ability to really go for it might be curtailed if you let your mind see monsters in the closet! Rather than miss out on life, you must fight back!

Start your day with the thought that you will stay positive regardless of what happens! Your attitude when leaving your bed as you wake up should be "I am ready to have an awesome day," not "Oh dear, it's morning, the day is starting." As Abraham Lincoln pointed out:

> *"Let no feeling of discouragement prey upon you, and in the end you are sure to succeed."*

Every day is like a diamond in the rough; it's up to you to polish the diamond and make it more brilliant!

Don't Worry About Situations—Deal With Them if They Arise

It is not constructive to keep worrying about a possible situation that may or may not arise. It is better to deal with the situation if and when it actually surfaces. Do not underestimate your own strength; when the situation calls, you will figure out what to do. You will have a response to deal with the situation. Period. No matter what life-problem happens, you will deal with it and the ways and means will present themselves. So, if you worry or become anxious, not only have you wasted your time and life worrying about something that might not happen, you have actually underestimated your ability to cope with the problem and overestimated the magnitude of the issue!

Perhaps you can sit down and start to think about the things that worry you and play out the scenario in your mind. Ask yourself, what's the worst that can happen? This time, play out your strategy to deal with it. After that, challenge your thought and remind yourself that what you are worrying about is not likely to happen! And, keep the worry to its proper size! You will feel a sense of control if you do this. Besides, as it has been often said, if you were to compare your problems with everyone else's, you would likely want to keep yours.

Never Lose Hope

Whoever has hope has everything. The worst thing one can do is to lose hope. It can be a slippery slope once hope is lost; you fall and getting up is pretty hard. Thankfully, getting up again is not impossible. But why go there? We cannot control everything in life. The weather is not in our control. The economy is not in our control. The affairs of the world are not in our control and how people treat us is not in our control. If we are more accepting that we are not able to control things, we can keep our selves away from undue worry or its evil cousin—depression. Keeping a spiritual focus can be a major source of strength in times that are difficult. In the Holy Qur'an we read:

> *"And when My servants ask thee about Me, say: 'I am near. I answer the prayer of the supplicant when he prays to Me. So they should hearken to Me and believe in Me, that they may follow the right way."* (2:187)

In Proverbs 24:14 we find:

"Know that wisdom is such to your soul; if you find it, there will be a future, and your hope will not be cut off."

From Mahatma Gandhi we learn:

"When doubts haunt me, when disappointments stare me in the face, and I see not one ray of hope on the horizon, I turn to Bhagavad Gita and find a verse to comfort me; and I immediately begin to smile in the midst of overwhelming sorrow. Those who meditate on the Gita will derive fresh joy and new meanings from it every day."

In other words, hope is paramount and keeping hope in your heart is the key to a worry-free life.

What We Can Learn from the Doberman
(Narrated by Ahsan)

Like most people, I always thought the Doberman was a ferocious guard dog that looked good from afar—very far. A few years ago, I was compelled to re-examine, or rather learn about the Doberman for the first time. It all happened as I was driving by a shopping plaza and saw a middle-aged woman with a beautiful black and rust Doberman. I literally stopped my car to have a closer look at the dog. It was a sunny day and the fur on this dog was shining. The dog was royal looking, an absolute stunner of grace and nobility. I never looked at dogs this way; I was just enamoured by this animal. Anyway, with the power of Google, I learned about this breed. Mr. Louis Doberman, a German police officer who was also a dog catcher, actually "invented" the dog in the late 1800s by cross-breeding several dogs to finally achieve what would become known as the Doberman. He wanted to breed a dog that would be fearless, intelligent, loyal, athletically proportioned and highly trainable. These are all qualities that any human being would like to possess let alone see in the "ultimate dog".

In the process of learning about the Doberman, I learned a bit about dogs in general. They have an innate quality that allows them to be aware of the emotions their owners are experiencing and will often help their owners to lift a low mood simply by snuggling up or demanding attention for play time. However it may be, dog owners are unanimous in their observation that their dogs teach them a very important lesson of life and that is to be like their dogs when it comes to staying in the moment. That is what dogs do. They are super unaware of dwelling on the past or focusing heavily on the future. The lesson we could all learn or remind ourselves is to be fearless, intelligent, loyal, athletically proportioned (as much as possible), highly trainable (as students of life) and stay in the moment. People who stay in the moment tend to worry less!

This is It!

You and I are not going to get a second chance to live this life. Knowing this, what do you choose for yourself—a life of worry and sitting on the side lines or a life of being carefree and sitting in the driver's seat? Life is happening and is beautiful. Enjoy each day as though it was your last, because one day it will be your last. Live life; love life.

We can also take inspiration from a Sanskrit poem of Kalidasa, a 5th century Hindu poet and playwright. He writes:

Look to this day for it is life, the very life of life.

In its brief course lie all the realities and verities of existence,
The bliss of growth—the splendour of action—the glory of power.
For yesterday is already a dream and tomorrow is only a vision,
But today—well lived—makes every yesterday a dream of happiness
And every tomorrow a vision of hope.
Look well, therefore, to this day!
Such is the salutation of this dawn.

Avoid Getting Stuck in Your Own Web

Be like a spider that does not get caught in its own web, the web representing the intricate fabric of life events and challenges that lay before you. In your own mind, you know that there are many things one could worry about; however, like a spider, you can walk across your web without getting stuck. Have you ever stopped to wonder how this feat is accomplished by the spider? The web has sticky threads that go around and around like a wheel and non-sticky threads that radiate from the centre like spokes. The design of the web and its stickiness will make other insects get stuck so the spider can eat its next meal, but the spider does not get stuck and walks along its web. The design of its feet is such that it has a special third claw that enables it to do so. You too have special abilities to navigate around the web of life and not get stuck. Use the ones that work for you, be it positive self-talk, staying busy, praying to your Creator, not giving up and pressing on, talking it out with a friend, looking at others who are in a greater bind like those in war-torn countries and on and on. Use those special capabilities, means and methods to walk and glide along towards your awesome life and tranquillity of mind.

Go Ahead, Worry—But Don't Despair

Here is a list of things you could worry about: losing your health; losing a loved one; losing the love of someone; losing your job; being harmed by a stranger; being broke; your business failing. You can probably add a few of your own, but these are the biggies. Regardless of any of the above worries or particular worry that is on one's mind, you may like to ask a powerful question: ***What are the chances that (the thing you fear or worry about) will happen?*** Another powerful question is, ***Where is the proof it will happen?*** Don't blow things out of proportion! It has been rightly said that 99% of what we worry about, never happens! When you see that a tough situation is upon you, be as calm as you can so that you can think about a solution. Rather than worry, get busy thinking, ***What do I do now?*** Be in a powerful state of mind. There is a solution and the feared outcome may never be as bad as imagined. Just remember this little gem:

> *"Life is like a camera—focus on what's important, capture the good times, develop from the negatives, and if things don't work out, take another shot."* Anonymous

Undoubtedly, we are not saying that problems and challenges won't arise in our lives. Bad things happen and good things happen. In fact, life is never a smooth ride. That's just life and knowing so may be all you need to accept that something out of the blue can come up. One can find evidence of this and comfort too when they read in the Holy Qur'an that:

"No soul is burdened beyond its capacity." (2:234), and

"We have surely created man to face hardships." (90:5), and

"And We will try you with something of fear and hunger, and loss of wealth and lives, and fruits; but give glad tidings to the patient who, when a misfortune overtakes them, say; 'Surely, to Allah we belong and to Him shall we return.' It is these on whom are blessings from their Lord and mercy and it is these who are rightly guided." (2:156-158)

The Prophet Muhammad[pbuh] also instructed us in the following Tradition:

"For a Muslim, life is full of good, and nobody but a true believer finds himself in that position, for if he meets with success he is grateful to God and becomes the recipient of greater favours from Him. On the other hand, if he suffers pain and tribulation, he endures it with patience and thus again makes himself deserving of God's favours."

We can also be delighted as we read in the Holy Qur'an,

"Surely there is ease after hardship." (24:6), and

"Allah will soon bring about ease after hardship." (65:8)

It is important to know that worry is a real emotion. It is only human. The anguish and loss it can produce is also real and not your destiny. Mahatma Gandhi said:

"There is nothing that wastes the body like worry, and one who has any faith in God should be ashamed to

worry about anything whatsoever."

Perhaps the most helpful strategy to employ regarding worry is the simple advice given by the Prophet Muhammad[pbuh], a man whose father died before he was born, who even lost his mother when he was just a child of six years, and, as a father, buried eleven of his own children. He suggested we start by looking at our situation compared to someone else who is experiencing an even worse loss or tragedy. This approach can instantly snap a person out of a feeling of worry or despair by changing their perspective. This comparison strategy acts as a soothing wake up call. Compared to others, our actual or imagined problems become less concerning.

Something Tragic Happened—Now What?

If you are facing a hard time and you are affected by a loss or tragedy, you have many choices to deal with your situation. Staying in the suffering mode is one choice, albeit, a disempowering one. You could also make a "comeback" by refusing to stay down or defining yourself by the awful thing that happened. Bounce back by talking out your feelings with your best friend or parent, by helping others who need help in your community, by staying busy with your work routine, by reading a book or watching a movie on the subject, by going for a walk every night to connect with yourself, by making yourself a priority and taking care of yourself. Keep in mind that there are support groups you could join and professionals you could seek out too, starting with a caring doctor, clergyman, or psychologist. Meeting with these professionals will benefit you because they have most likely dealt with hundreds of people with the exact thing you are going through. Take advantage of knowledge, their knowledge.

You can't be an expert on everything. Mind you, the

end game will be that it will be up to you to shift your thinking. Let's take a moment to remember we are thinking beings; our thoughts produce feelings and emotions. Based on those feelings and emotions, we dare or don't dare to make changes in life—actions in life—or even try at all. If this is true and you believe it to be true, your best strategy is to focus on your thoughts and get them to be of a nature that brings you to a level of emotion somewhat better than before. You can then take a baby step towards an action you know will be a step in the right direction. No one can actually do this for you; yes, he can counsel you, he can show you by example, he can meet you once a week, he can feel for you, but only you can do what you must do!

Having relied on yourself and others to help you through, always remember to have faith that your Creator is there for you. We can be encouraged when we read in the Bhagavad Gita:

> *"On this path effort never goes to waste, and there is no failure. Even a little effort toward spiritual awareness will protect you from the greatest fear."*

You will need a resolute mental focus to overcome your adversity and you will need the aid of prayer. There is a three part "declaration" you can make if you please, in addition to your formal daily prayer: I believe in Allah (God), I trust in Allah, I do not worry. Try it on for size as you deal with your "temporary" fear or worry. If your loved one is late for example, your thoughts should not be that something bad has happened (catastrophizing). In fact, most people don't think like this! Instead, know that dozens of reasons can cause a delay: traffic, a last-minute business phone call, a flat tire, stopping off to buy milk. Besides, you should relinquish this responsibility of protecting your family to God; no amount of worrying about What Ifs will make any difference. Our protector is God Himself and understanding this brings peace to one's mind. No news is good news.

Know that your thoughts are controllable. You have dominion over your thoughts. This is a sign of strength. The undisciplined mind is not strength. As Gautama Buddha said:

> *"We are what we think. All that we are arises with our thoughts. With our thoughts, we make the world."*

Apply discipline to your thinking and banish the monsters to the place they really belong—the garbage can—not in your head or under your bed.

Menu of Worry Extinguishers

Always remember that life **will** present you with challenges. However, a setback, if viewed as a set up for a comeback, means that the best is yet to come! Now that you know that you need to be aware of your worry and put it into context. Now that you know that any problem or challenge you face will also give birth to a solution and means to cope with it. Now that you know that you can control your thoughts and that prayer is your fortification, what practical daily strategies can you implement? The following are some strategies to banish your worries. Literally tell your intruding thought to **stop** and **go away**! Or, say to yourself a simple thing such as, "I can do this". Or, recall a time that you were successful to boost your confidence and belief. Also, putting yourself into the so-called uncomfortable situation in a "baby steps" way will boost your belief. Amaze yourself and be a bit bolder than before.

Focus on positive thoughts and refuse to be a negative thinker. Sometimes your negative thoughts can inadvertently manifest negative outcomes. Be careful!

Literally turn off incoming messages that are negative, such as radio commercials about personal injury lawsuits, debt relief and bankruptcy services. Don't click open articles that are sensational and alarming. Boycott negative chatter, period.

Keep in mind that you are not a static unchanging person. You are ever improving and ever changing. Don't doubt this! You are not the same person of even three years ago. A lot has happened in the last three years and you have learned many things and you are not the same person therefore. Base your thoughts on what is real not imagined.

Stay Calm and Breathe

Need more ideas? Consider this breathing exercise, which is quite valuable and will bring a feeling of physical relaxation if your mind or heart is pumping. Try this now: take in a deep breath for three counts and hold it for three counts and then release the breath for a controlled three counts. Repeat. Repeat again. Any time you need to quickly snap yourself back to a feeling of calm and centeredness, do this breathing routine. For even more meditative breathing and relaxation, try to make a goal of breathing deeply for ten minutes a day. Build up to this time by doing it for at least three minutes on your first try. Although you can do this at any place or time during the day, like while you are driving to work, an excellent place and time to do this is just as you lie down to sleep. Focus on your breathing so that your belly and lower rib cage is expanding. Breathe in deliberately and slowly, but deep breaths. Feel yourself sinking into your bed, with your shoulders relaxing. Get in touch with the sensation as you breathe that your neck, back, arms and legs are melting into the bed. Think of just these thoughts (the breathing and the relaxation of your body). Doing this is easy for you. Breathe yourself into a nice deep sleep.

Refuse to Label Yourself

In addition to these ideas, use the "fake it till you make it" technique. This is simply acting as if you are not scared. By being bolder in your approach even when your knees are shaking a bit you will, over time, get yourself to a point where your fear thought or worry is a thing of the past. This will be true for you, because you will reflect on your past accomplishments and become stronger! Those who generally worry can also try staying focused on being in one room all the time. Metaphorically, people sit in a room that has two doors, one that leads into the room and one that leads out of the room. The trick is to lock both doors, the one that opens up the past and the one that opens up the future. Now, you are in one room and can focus on enjoying the "**now**". This is the best room to be in, so you can live in the moment and smell the aroma of fine cooking; the smile of your child; a piece of art on your book shelf; the sun rising; the majesty of the mountains, the sounds of the wind blowing through the trees on a fall afternoon or the sweetness of connecting to your Creator in prostration during prayer. The famous American philosopher and psychologist William James has remarked:

"The greatest discovery of my generation is that a human being can alter his life by altering his attitudes."

He also said: *"If you want a quality, act as if you already had it."*

Perhaps, all you have to do is say, "I don't worry about anything; I am not a worrier!"

Get Out of Your Head

Some people over-think. They have a lot of time on

their hands too. Ultimately, this is a bad habit. If you are caught up in a mental loop, consider the strategies discussed in this chapter. Most importantly, know that you can always change a habit even if it's a habit of thinking a certain way. A baby born today in the developed countries, especially in the USA or Canada, lives better than kings of 150 years ago and has the most opportunities of any child the world over! We live in an era of great possibilities and promise. Things are getting better the world over in general, so why should you be left out? In short, anxiety lives in the past and the future. Don't jump to conclusions based on limited information and don't get stuck. Change your internal dialogue from What If? to Come What May, I Will be OK! Live in the moment and remember what Mark Twain said:

> *"I spent a lot of time worrying about things most of which never happened!"*

Transformation requires right thinking, so fill your mind with thoughts of courage, patience, tranquillity of spirit, self-reliance, cheerfulness, steadfastness, contentment and optimism. And finally, remember that you must rely on yourself with certain faith that your true Helper, Sustainer, Nourisher and Source of peace is your God whom you ask each and every day for guidance. As it says in the Holy Qur'an:

> *"...It is in the remembrance of Allah that hearts can find comfort."* (13:29)

Advice from a Chinese Farmer

Try to remember the following story for good measure. An ancient Chinese farmer had one son and one horse. One day his horse ran away and his neighbours came over to console him, saying how unfortunate this was. His means of farming and income disappeared overnight. The farmer was not happy but his reply was, "Maybe it is bad, let us see." Then the next day, the horse returned and brought with it two more female horses! The neighbours came over to rejoice with the farmer and the farmer said "Maybe it is good, let us see." The following day, his son fell off one of the new horses and broke his leg! The neighbours came to comfort the farmer as his only son and support was injured. The old man looked at them and exclaimed, "Maybe this is bad, let us see." Not a day later, a life-changing event swept over the village when the Emperor's Army came through and all the village's young men and boys were taken to fight a war. The old farmer's son was left because of his broken leg! A wise man once stated that when you look back over the events of your life and connect the dots you will often be amazed to see the bright side of what at the time looked to be huge problem.

To rephrase the famous quote by Ralph Waldo Emerson:

> *"Remember that for each minute that you spend worrying, you may be losing sixty seconds of happiness."*

Action Steps

1. What point from the preceding paragraphs really resonates with you at this time in your life?
2. What worry or anxiety do you want to deal with once and for all?
3. What inspiring story or person can you think of that would strengthen your resolve?
4. What virtue of character do you want to cultivate? Courage? Self-control? Optimism?

5. What friend will you enlist for help?
6. Recall a time in your life when you achieved a goal or overcame a difficulty. Feel the feelings you experienced then. See in your mind's eye a vivid picture of that moment or incident. Now keep this feeling and picture in your back pocket. Pull it out the next time you feel flustered!
7. Are your worries or concerns just First World issues? Do they compare to someone living in the Third World contending with food shortages, hungry babies, unclean water, civil war, kidnappings, disease and general lack of personal security? Many people won the lottery of life and don't even realize it.
8. How long do you think making a change in your thinking or your attitude requires?
9. Make a list of how you will enjoy life more because you no longer worry.

Chapter 8
Meditation and Mindfulness

"I just saved 100% on stress by switching to not giving a damn!"
Anonymous

"Do your best and forget the rest!"
Tony Horton

"Keep calm and read this chapter!"
Ahsan and Shazad

The world we live in today is fast paced and different from even thirty years ago. If you have any recollection of what life was like before email, faxes, cellphones, computers, the Internet, sixty-hour work weeks, working from home, quarterly performance appraisals, multi-tasking, after-school extra-curricular activities, continuing education requirements, upgrading and big-box shopping stores, you will likely agree. If we lived in simpler times the stress of daily life would be present, but not as ***intense***. To be realistic, we should take a moment to accept that we are not going to change the fast pace of the world, we can only condition our response to it. Meditation is an effective technique to use to do this. In this chapter, we will try to explain how to meditate; just be still and patient for a moment or two.

Mind Your Stress

What tools or methods could we employ to beat stress? The good news is that there are effective tools available. All of them will affect the one place that we experience stress first and foremost and that is in our minds. The mind is a powerful thing and it can work for us or against us, as discussed elsewhere in this book. Here is what makes it so influential to our experience of life. What we focus our mind on becomes what we see in our everyday life. In other words, frantic thinking will produce jittery feelings and unease in the mind and body. That feeling could be described as stress, anxiety, low energy or off mood. Being in a stressed state makes a person less effective and a misery for those around him.

Repeat After Me

So, when we refer to the mind, what do we mean exactly? There is our conscious mind and our subconscious mind. The conscious mind seems to be our thinking and experience part of the mind, whereas the subconscious mind governs and stores the overflow of information we gather from the world in the form of thoughts, experiences, memories, and ideas, and feeds these things to the conscious mind. In other words, the stored information in the subconscious mind can influence the awareness of the conscious mind and our resulting frame of mind.

In order to calm the conscious mind we can train our subconscious mind by repeating and concentrating on an empowering thought! For example, a person who is always feeling stressed out and irritable can declare that he is a calm person. This declaration's wording must be in the present tense. To make this technique effective you would not say "I will try to be calm", or "I can be calm"; you have to say it as though it is true right now! You will need to start each day by repeating this aloud 25-50 times. Although, this sounds excessive and you will feel silly, it will start to take effect. You will also need to repeat this exercise at least two more times during the same day, say in the mid afternoon and just as you fall asleep. In one day, you will have programmed your subconscious mind with an empowering thought 150 times! Over one week you will have achieved 1050 times! The next day, you will do the same, and the day after that you will do the same. If you do it for 30 days and you are not changed, do it for another 30 days. At some point, this positive declaration will be etched into that part of your mind be it the subconscious, the unconscious or the back of your mind and you will be completely transformed.

Whereas once you were prone to being stressed and irritable; now you will not be. Using this same technique, you could then move on to the next "quality" you want to improve in yourself. The mind is a powerful thing and the sooner you realize that your life and how much you enjoy it is mostly governed by your thoughts, habits, beliefs, values, internalized patterns, most of which should be challenged for their validity and usefulness, the sooner you will live in a reality that you create on purpose. You know people who are like this—perhaps you are one of them. The person who realizes that she has the power to control her mind's steering wheel lives a life of greater ease and joy, and not only for herself. If you are the best you can be, you not only benefit yourself but all those around you too.

Meditation vs. Prayer

As we just covered, if we try, we can condition our nature and mind to be resilient and serve our desired outcomes. When you repeat your declarations over and over, you will turn positive thinking into positive transformation. Aside from this approach or technique, two other methods of becoming peaceful and transforming towards one's desired results have been practiced since time immemorial: meditation and prayer. Which one is more effective? Which one is easier? Which one will deliver the result you are looking for?

When a mystic retreats into the forest and returns after

fifteen days of meditation, he will achieve calmness, a disciplined mind, relaxation and transformation. His results will make him very effective as a human being and all those around him will notice a beneficial change in him and will likewise benefit from his changes. The mystic may come up short, however, in one area if he also desires that. Here, we mean one's personal relationship and connection to his Creator. The deepest level of connection and relationship that a person can achieve with his Creator comes from one's efforts in prayer. It is through prayer in the state of certainty that God exists, hears and responds to his prayers that an average Joe, let alone a mystic, will drink the syrup of the most profound peace one will ever know. Through the ages men and women of all religions and traditions have practiced this technique, called prayer. In a nutshell, there are two ways of executing this strategy: the first is to practice meditation; the other is to just ask God to give you the outcome you desire by trusting Him. This way, what is hidden from you becomes shown to you, and the means to achieve your ends become apparent.

Meditation 101

Meditation is an excellent practice in which to engage. It is an advanced means of self-awareness and a means to calm the central nervous system. It does not need to be associated with any religious tradition and is sometimes referred to as mindfulness. Meditation as a practice can also reprogram your thoughts towards your goals. It is essential to do it consistently, starting with five minutes daily and working up from there. So, how does one do it?

First and foremost, you will need to schedule it into your day and create a relaxed and unplugged environment. You could jump right into it or better yet, do some light yoga exercise first for at least five minutes. The benefit of stretching first will be to loosen up the tension in your body and this will make your meditation easier to achieve. A personal friend describes how he spends 45 minutes in total, usually in the morning, where he does his yoga first and ends it with a 20-minute meditation. He has rarely missed a day in the last 50 years and says he has felt great for those years because he practices this discipline daily.

Once you have done some physical moves to loosen up, find a comfortable place to sit; you could use a chair with a firm back rest or you could sit cross-legged (comfortably not in a pretzel unless you can) on the floor, with your spine straight. This position of being straight will be important, because meditation requires correct breathing. If you are hunched forward in a lazy posture, your breath will be restricted and the benefits eliminated. Next, close your eyes and start to breathe deeply. As you know, we tend to breathe shallow breaths whereas in your meditation session, you will focus on a deep belly breath. Breathe in from your nose and let your belly expand like a balloon. Then exhale from your nose and deliberately keep on exhaling until you feel you let the last bit of air come out. By exhaling fully, you will automatically trigger a deep breath. Keep doing your deep breathing as best as you can. You can start off with a five-minute session and work up from there. Some people meditate for long periods and others short; however, like anything else, it should be done daily to create maximum effect.

So, sitting in a quiet space with your eyes closed and breathing deeply is the skill you need to practice first. Next, is to clear your mind of mental chatter and intrusive thoughts. It will be hard to do, because your inner voice is with you all day and never shuts up. If you are thinking about the guy who cut you off on the street or about a school or work project, you will not achieve the relaxation that a good meditation session is supposed to give you. This is where most people give up, because they find it impossible to think about nothing. For most of us, thinking about nothing is not going to happen so to combat this, every time a silly thought comes through your mind, observe it and let it go rather than think more about it. Let it pass through your mind without dwelling on it. Instead just focus on the feeling of your breathing (the in breath and the out breath going through your nose and expanding the belly); this should keep unnecessary thoughts from galloping through your mind. Don't worry about thinking about nothing; if you can't block your thoughts, so be it. Like all things in life, stick with it. You will not become an expert right away. If you work at it, you will gain its benefits. This discipline of meditation should be viewed as a way to be aware of staying in the moment and not stressing about the future or even the past.

Meditation is a good thing. Saints and prophets all engaged in some form of meditation; you can develop your own as you wish. Meditation can be viewed as an additional tool in your tool box that supplements but does not supplant prayer. For many in the world, their prayer is their meditation and for them, that is all they need. For others, meditation is their prayer. The lines seem to blur, but one thing is clear: regardless of what you call it, having a conversation with the Creator, knowing that He exists and hears you, brings real peace and steadfastness in the ups and downs of life.

Prayer 101

So how should we pray? Is there a special technique? Your prayer method will likely be more familiar to you, as you would have grown up praying according to your religious tradition. The way you pray is your personal matter. That said, here are a few concepts to try on for size. Rather than praying for all the things on your wish list, focus your prayer on gratitude to God for all the things you have in your life. This gratitude list will remind you of all that you have going for you and put you in a wonderful and uplifted emotional state. The Sufis (a mystical component of Islam) prayed in such a way that they were extremely grateful for the things most of us take for granted. They were grateful for being alive, for having food to eat, for having a family to love, for having a livelihood. Another aspect of their prayer was to pray for nearness to God by asking God to make their heart so clean that He would descend into it. In addition to this, you can ask God to give you wisdom rather than material things. These approaches to prayer help one to have respect for God and foster more love in one's heart for God. Ultimately, these efforts lead to increased peace, joy and steadfastness. It has been said that if you start to pray regularly and with concentration, you will bring about a revolution within yourself; a whole change in yourself will manifest.

Power of Prayer

Prayer can be your ultimate tool because it gives you instant relief. The result of sincere prayer is tranquillity of mind and true happiness. You gain another worldly strength to deal with the problem you are praying about and you are better able to deal with it. Even if your prayer is not answered right away, or at all, you develop patience and resolve to endure your challenges. Rather than worry, you are in a state of positive expectation that either the solution will appear or you will be able to handle the problem regardless. Prayer becomes a way of forging a relationship with God and knowing that He is also your most loyal and loving Friend: a Friend whom you can truly adore and devote yourself to, a Friend whose qualities are praiseworthy and awe inspiring.

We have only so many days in our lives, so why not enjoy every day to the fullest? Why be relaxed only now and then? Perhaps we can reject the idea that you can't be calm and relaxed every day and that some suffering is inevitable. What if even in the midst of problems or a rough patch in life, we remind ourselves of our blessings and use the strategy of prayer so that we obtain peace and security of mind? What is inevitable is that problems will crop up but your reaction to them is your choice. You can be like the sea hawk and soar above them with a developed response of steadfastness or react to them like an aimless rubber ducky. The choice is yours; the choice is always yours.

Action Steps

1. In addition to reciting your declarations throughout the day, write them out. Get a notebook and write out your declarations several times each morning or evening. The act of writing and focusing on the words as you do will have a powerful effect of etching your desired outcome in your mind and cause you to do what you need to do.

2. Look at your environment and try to get the stressors out of your life. Say no to a few projects; take a day off each week to recharge your batteries. Plan some activity that gives you relaxation. Unplug from the online world.

3. Make a list of 50 things you are grateful for. Type out a final copy in a nice font and frame it so you can view it daily. This will bring you feelings of serenity and appreciation.

4. Set aside 10 to 30 minutes each day to pray, meditate or be mindful. Don't skip a day.

5. Take a measurement of your stress levels before and after you pray or meditate.

6. Set up a weekly meeting with a friend and report to him or her on the things you did over the last week to make your life awesome and serene.

7. When meditating, focus your attention on connecting with yourself; when praying, focus your conversation and concentration on connecting with your Friend.

8. Be patient when beseeching answers to your prayers. Your job is to pray and not to give up.

9. Encourage your loved ones to consider these techniques so that they, too, will know their benefits.

Chapter 9
Happy Marriage

"Love is patient and kind; love does not envy or boast; it is not arrogant or rude. It does not insist on its own way; it is not irritable or resentful; it does not rejoice at wrongdoing, but rejoices with the truth. Love bears all things, believes all things, hopes all things, endures all things."
1 Corinthians 13:4-7

"Steadfast love and faithfulness meet; righteousness and peace kiss each other."
Psalm 85:10

"My wife tells me that if I ever decide to leave, she is coming with me."
Jon Bon Jovi

Marriage is a very interesting state of existence. Those who have been at it for a length of time will attest that it is something that has to be valued and worked on to make it a state of joy. Anyone who is married will offer great advice on how to keep your marriage working at optimum. The point to keep in mind is that marriage is a voluntary situation. One chooses to be married and one chooses to make their marriage the best it can be. The special twist, however, is that marriage is a situation in which a husband cannot make the decision about a happy marriage on his own exclusively and neither can his wife. This has to be a common goal and a shared vision between the two.

Be Serious About Your Marriage Success

Perhaps, and this is all we can conjecture, the main

reason a marriage leads to cohabitation hell or worse—divorce—is a lack of seriousness at the outset. The attitude of a student who takes a course with the thought that "If it is not to my liking, I will drop it" is a very close parallel. So is the person who starts a job or starts a business and drops it at the first sign of challenge. Likewise, the person who enters a marriage with a throw-away, disposable or non-committal attitude is not necessarily going to make their marriage the "important" part of their life that it is supposed to be. Marriage success is at least as important as any other major goal or project that a person takes on in other areas of their life. In fact, a happy marriage is a major source of comfort and fuel that ripples across other areas of our life. When your married life is good, your health is good. When married life is good, your kids feel secure. When married life is good, your performance on the job and in your business is accelerated. When married life is good, your spirit is lifted, your countenance is brighter, your outlook is limitless and your sense of purpose is heightened. The converse is also unfortunately true.

Love is like air, you need it to live. As we learn from Lao Tzu:

> *"To love someone deeply gives you strength. Being loved by someone deeply gives you courage."*

Stop Trying to Change One Another

That said, what can be done to assure great success in marriage and therefore more enjoyment out of life? You need to have one thing straight in your mind. No two people can ever be the same, we all have certain unique personality traits and that's okay! It's not realistic or probable that your spouse is the mirror image of yourself, meets all your expectations, and acts in complete harmony with your moods. So, if no two people are the same, accept this reality and try to make your marriage about things you share in common and focus on those, rather than trying to make your better half a person who is more likeable to you. Focus also on your common vision of life and your goals as a couple. The more you try to make your spouse someone you think they should be, the more you will drive a wedge between yourselves—period. Sorry, this had to be said.

Despite this crazy truth of being two different people, you can definitely make your marriage a model for the ages and a source of peace and contentment for you and your family. The guidance that we find in the Holy Qur'an that describes the role of spouses is:

> *"...They are a garment for you, and you are a garment for them..."* (2:188)

In other words, just like clothing, a husband and wife are to be a means of protection, loveliness and a source of comfort to each other. We can aspire to protect our spouse in every way possible, making their lives as happy as can be. We can bring out the beauty of potential in our spouse by helping them to achieve their goals in life. We can be there for our spouse through good times and bad to help them feel appreciated and secure.

Men and Women are Different—Don't You Know?

It might also be worth noting that men and women are different in how they think and feel about certain subjects. You might expect that your husband is as nurturing and loving as you are and that he ought to show it in the same way that you do. For example, you might think he should say he loves you more often, be a bit more affectionate with you, be even more thoughtful and know your feelings without you verbalizing them. If you were to ask him why he comes up short on this, you would find that his thinking is not what you perceive. Most assuredly, he would think the following: I do my part by earning money and I cut the lawn last week, plus I do love you and told you that sometime last year. Besides, what am I—a mind reader? Not to say that this thinking is correct, but that's not too far from the truth on how he thinks. Now, if you don't get it and think he's an oaf and a tyrant, your level of marital bliss will be affected that day for sure. Likewise, a man does not necessarily understand that you are hinting at something that is bothering you and that you expect him to know what you want from him even though you have not told him. He thinks you are being emotional and would rather you told him straight up what's on your mind. After all, that's how his best friend deals with him, and so does his brother and so does his barber. Perhaps knowing that we think differently from each other would at least explain why sometimes we are at odds with each other, and think of each other as odd!

The smart thing for men and women to do is to think of their differences as something that is baked in the cake, it's our nature to be different from each other. If we understand that we are different in our emotional sensitivity, different in our attention to details, different in our way of expressing love and affection, or different in our likes and dislikes, we would avoid big arguments. We would also avoid marital discord, which, if left unaddressed, results in divorce. We literally have to adopt a different attitude and way of approach to each other. Men, you might need to do more than throw out the garbage. In fact doing dishes now and then may earn you points in other ways (nudge, nudge, wink, wink). Women, you might encourage your husband to go out with the boys at least once or twice a week, so you have a more balanced husband. Try this and see it work. It will work. Bumping heads does not work.

Close, but Not Too Close

Marriage is supposed to bring you and your spouse closer together. However, there is danger in having a relationship so close that you stifle each other. Each one of you needs to grow, flourish and put out roots and branches and, much like two trees that are growing near each other, it is important to leave enough space in between. This thought is beautifully represented by Khalil Gibran (1883-1931), a Lebanese-American philosopher poet and writer, in the following poem:

"Love One Another"

You were born together, and together you shall be forever more.
You shall be together when the white wings of death scatter your days.
Ay, you shall be together even in the silent memory of God.
But let there be spaces in your togetherness,
And let the winds of the heavens dance between you.

Love one another, but make not a bond of love:
Let it rather be a moving sea between the shores of your souls.
Fill each other's cup, but drink not from one cup.
Give one another of your bread, but eat not from the same loaf.
Sing and dance together and be joyous, but let each of you be alone,
Even as the strings of a lute are alone though they quiver with the same music.

Give your hearts, but not into each other's keeping.
For only the hand of Life can contain your hearts.
And stand together yet not too near together:
For the pillars of the temple stand apart,
And the oak tree and the cypress grow not in each other's shadow.

Say No Evil, See No Evil

Come closer if you want to hear the best marital advice ever. Here it is: Men, keep your tongue silent when you see your wife upset and sharing her view in a louder tone than normal. This is not the time to lose your cool. From experience, you know what you might say will have little benefit at best and could be misinterpreted very easily. Women, look the other way. Don't let your eyes be on the constant lookout for things that your husband does that need to be fixed. Sometimes, ignoring what you see and addressing it later when you are not irked is the best strategy. You can still achieve your objective and avoid an argument. It can go both ways; both men and women need to be mindful of the above. Be less nit-picky and less dramatic with each other and watch how your marriage becomes a source of lasting happiness in life.

Lower Your Standards

In other words, don't expect perfection in your mate and don't become easily annoyed or frustrated. Neither husbands nor wives are perfect and will never be perfect and you knew this before you married. You are married for a reason: to enjoy all the best of life with a constant partner and comforter. Somehow you will make it work at the level you choose by thinking of what is best for both of you (which may mean compromising and seeing the other point of view). Think happy marriage and you will have one; think awful marriage and you will have one. Rather than be easily roused by emotions and ego, be easy-going like a stream flowing down a mountain, reaching its destination. The wise counsel of Benjamin Franklin should be noted well by both men and women:

"Keep your eyes wide open before marriage, half shut afterwards."

Be Cheerful and Happy in the First Place

Here is a real story: an older gentleman of seventy years or so walks into his dry cleaner and is greeted by the owner, who happens to be a middle-aged woman. After their greetings to each other, the gentleman makes a comment about his wife regarding how she is easily upset by small things and gets and stays in a bad mood. The owner remarks that she is always in a good mood, because she is grateful for the day she has today and that she knows tomorrow is guaranteed to no one. She even says that she loves her husband and feels he is the best husband she could ever have. You could be the grouchy husband or you could be the grouchy wife, but if you think like the dry cleaner, you would likely move your married life towards a better place. And yes, both partners need to think like the dry cleaner. You cannot clap with one hand.

Don't be a Mama's Boy

Many marriages are influenced by interfering mothers-in-law. For some reason, the mother of the man feels that the new woman is not good enough for her son and is perhaps jealous that she is second in line for her son's attention. The son is often caught in the middle between his mother who complains about her incompetent and unworthy daughter-in-law and his wife, who complains about the mother-in-law's criticisms. What is a son to do? What is a husband to do? He has to be firm and create some mutual understanding between the two important women in his life. He should never take sides and he should never come under the influence of either so as to let his marriage become affected or destroyed. If possible, a mother-in-law should stay out of her son's marriage regardless of her feelings stated above. If possible, the daughter in-law should stay calm about the situation so as not to fuel the fire. As long as the son rises above the situation and balances out the drama, he should remain married and not get written out of his mother's will.

You Have One of Two Choices

A wise father gave his son some excellent marriage advice on his wedding day. He told his son what he had experienced, as the ultimate wisdom about marriage: "You have one of two choices in your marriage: either be right or be happy." If you and your spouse reflect on this, you will likely reframe your thoughts the next time some "issue" comes up. He further told his son that he always chose to be happy and that's why he never got into any serious fight with his own wife. If you wish to be happy, this will mean that you might have to ignore your foot getting stepped on once in a while.

A further concept to adopt is that you are coming across to your spouse a certain way at any given moment and likewise she is coming across a certain way to you. Your interpretation of what she is doing or thinking may be correct and it might be incorrect. For example, you might feel that your spouse is being uncooperative about helping out in the house, when in fact she is distracted by certain pressures at work. Rather than jump to conclusions, take time to clarify what is going on and always think about throwing your frustrations overboard. Just remind yourself of your goal of being happy rather than right! Together, you should wipe away frustrations and think about the greater goal of your happy life.

Furthermore, when you need to "discuss" things, always use the best language and manners with each other. Your spouse deserves your respect and reverence, not a sharp tongue. It has been said that mean words are like nails hammered into a piece of wood. Those words can be taken back by apologizing for them, but think of what is left after the apology. The nails or words were pulled out of the piece of wood, but the marks are there forever!

The Story of the Perfect Marriage

Once upon a time, there were two people who married. They loved each other immensely, had deep respect for each other, and did not try to change each other's personalities. They lived happily together and in time were blessed with many children. Raising a family became their priority, but they also made some personal time for each other, so that they would continue to grow forward together rather than grow apart. When their children grew up and started their own families, the couple's love matured into an even better kind of mutual respect and tenderness than their first years of marriage. Together, they enjoyed life with each other and their family. They did separate eventually when one of them left the world. The surviving spouse had fond memories and thanked God for having the good fortune of living with their life partner as long as they did. The surviving partner yearned to be reunited in heaven when the time would eventually come. Does it get any better than this? Is this not how things ought to be?

Marriage Advice from the Holy Qur'an

The guidance on marriage in the Qur'an is very inspiring:

> *"And of His Signs is that He has created wives for you from among yourselves that you may find peace of mind in them, and He has put love and tenderness between you. In that, surely, are Signs for a people who reflect."* (30:22)

"He it is Who created you from a single soul and made therefrom its mate, that he might find comfort in her." (7:190)

"Our Lord, grant us of our wives and children the delight of our eyes, and make us a model for the righteous." (25:75)

From the verses above, an ideal marriage should be a mutual source of love and tenderness, peace of mind, and a source of comfort and delight and happiness. Let this be a source of inspiration and a goal for us all to achieve in our marriage.

The Prophet Muhammad[pbuh] has mentioned that the best among you is the one who treats his wife the best. In fact, his own home life was spent in keeping company with his wives and helping them in the daily domestic chores of the house. Think about that for a minute.

He has also said that women should be treated like glass. That is to say, that glass is fragile and should not be handled harshly. A proper way to behave with one's wife would be along this ideal and not to think of her as your subordinate. She is not.

Happiness in marriage, as in all other situations, has to be earned with hard work and perseverance. As the Dalai Lama once remarked:

"Happiness is not something readymade. It comes from your own actions."

Fifty Awesome Marriage Tips

Here then is a list of tips to keep your marriage happy:

1. Listen to your spouse.

2. Love each other and consider each other as persons with unique identities.
3. Pray for God to increase your love for each other
4. Forgive each other's faults.
5. Forget and move on; never bring up the past.
6. Respect each other's families and never talk about them in a disparaging way.
7. Don't ruminate or dwell on things.
8. Be patient with each other.
9. Put your faith in God that things are moving in the right direction.
10. Be flexible and be willing to bend a little for each other.
11. Under no circumstances let your home become a stressful atmosphere.
12. Never be dramatic and loud in front of your children.
13. Lose the drama with each other.
14. Be romantic.
15. Dress up and smell good for your spouse; be neat and clean in your appearance every day.
16. Think of each other's feelings.
17. Touch base during the day.
18. Focus on your friendship.
19. Have fun and laugh together.
20. Keep realistic expectations of each other.
21. Be conservative with spending money and don't accumulate excessive debt.
22. Hold hands in public.
23. Don't hurt each other's feelings and don't raise your voice.
24. Never go to bed angry.
25. Keep communications open and respectful.
26. Give compliments to each other.
27. Accept compliments from each other.
28. Joke around and be cheerful.

29. Love each other unconditionally.
30. Set up a regular date night.
31. Talk about the future together.
32. Find a hobby to share together such as gardening, hiking, camping, golfing, photography, cooking or _______.
33. Encourage your spouse to enjoy his or her favourite hobby or pastime.
34. Go on a vacation for two weeks without the kids; Paris and London are calling!
35. Go on a mini two-day vacation.
36. Be spontaneous.
37. Anticipate each other's wants and needs.
38. Pray together.
39. Get some marriage counselling.
40. Hug each other throughout the day.
41. Pick your battles.
42. Write a love letter and put it in a place for your spouse to find as a surprise.
43. Be encouraging in your words and be your spouse's cheerleader.
44. Call each other by a "special" name that you only use for each other and no one else.
45. Look at your spouse when they don't notice it and just gaze.
46. Spend a little time asking your spouse how her day went.
47. Make your spouse a cup of tea or coffee without him asking for it.
48. Do some housework to lighten your spouse's load.
49. Give your spouse a shoulder massage.
50. Tell your spouse you love her.

The list you see is not an exhaustive and conclusive list; so add to it here.

Action Steps

1. Make a pledge that your marriage is an important aspect of life and discuss what each of you values in the marriage. Your goal should be that your married life is a source of lasting peace and happiness.
2. Have regular discussions with your spouse about how you feel your marriage is going. Then get busy working on yourself, don't tell your spouse that they need to get better for your marriage to be a happier one.
3. Make the success of your marriage one of the values you focus on in your life, so your spouse is on the same page as you.
4. Share your other goals in life with each other and make a plan to help each other achieve them. Who better a life coach than your spouse? Who better a cheerleader or accountability partner? Remember what happened in the film *Rocky* when Adrian told Rocky to "win".
5. Have faith and pray together for the outcomes you desire in your family life, both today and for the future. Your bond with God will improve as will your bond with each other and your children.
6. Focus on the success and quality of your married life and your kids will automatically benefit. They receive the blessing of growing up in a home that feels secure and peaceful, free of shouting matches and tension.
7. Plan a surprise "special day" for your spouse based on her favourite place to go, restaurant or favourite activity. Do this a few times a year. Imagine if someone did that for you?
8. Pull out your calendar now and schedule in a

vacation for just the two of you. Being together in an airplane and sipping coffee is good for you both, let alone savouring a romantic dinner in a foreign city or staring at the Mona Lisa and holding hands.

9. We all are very busy, and missing each other like two passing ships is very common for many couples. Try to sit together daily, even for fifteen minutes to ask about each other's day over a cup of tea.
10. Create memories because in reality you are living together on borrowed time; you never know when one of you might leave this world.

Chapter 10
Public Speaking

"Speech is power: speech is to persuade, to convert, to compel." Ralph Waldo Emerson

"Gracious words are like a honeycomb, sweetness to the soul and health to the body." Proverbs 16:24

"Ask not what your country can do for you, ask what you can do for your country." John F. Kennedy

He who can communicate well and get his point across to others is not only admired by others, but also breathes a rarefied air. Such a person is considered a leader. Often, he is successful. Many of them are involved in important roles and careers. These people seem to walk on water. Okay, maybe they can't actually walk on water, but they seem to be able to do what many people are afraid to do. Studies say the biggest fear that most people have is to give a talk in front of an audience; public speaking to them is as scary as furry little spiders are to arachnophobes.

How to be an Awesome Speaker

Being an accomplished speaker, even a plain speaker, is a coveted position. But what if you feel that this goal is too daunting? How do you climb this personal Mount Everest? Here is a powerful suggestion: try! Speaking confidently in public will make you part of an exclusive club. These are people who at one point were not public speakers (think leaders, successful, amazing humans) because great speakers are not born, they are developed. Don't let fear of being laughed at or failure stop you. All speakers, even "pros", have butterflies in their stomach just before starting their speech. What they learned over time is that the nervousness goes away after the first few sentences. Every one of them started off at level one and then ascended rapidly to higher and higher levels. If you are a student reading this book and you are thinking about reaching the top of your chosen profession, you **must** become a good speaker. You will distinguish yourself from the rest of your peers, and you will earn considerably more, because you will be identified as more competent and talented.

In other words, with practice, an average Joe or Jill who has the gift of speech walks around with a halo. Becoming a speaker is not only a worthy goal, but is also easy. However, you still have to do the following: try! As F. Scott Fitzgerald, author of *The Great Gatsby*, said:

> *"Genius is the ability to put into effect what is on your mind."*

In a nutshell, speaking in front of people can be summarized as follows: Know your audience, paint a picture of what you are about to say, speak to them in a way that respects them and informs them of something they want to know, summarize what you said to them before you conclude your speech, answer questions for three to five minutes after your powerful closing points and sit down. Job done.

Help Your Audience to Understand You

When you address any size audience, keep in mind that your "communication" is not a two-way responsibility. That is to say, your listeners are not responsible for understanding you. Rather, as a speaker, you have a responsibility to make sure, what you are saying is being understood by your audience. The delivery of the topic of your speech needs to be custom-tailored to the listeners. If you talk over their heads by getting "technical" or fail to keep a clear path for them to follow as you develop your points, you will not only lose them, they will never thank you for speaking. In fact, if you speak and get people saying thanks at the end of your speech, you know you have done a great job. So, as you write your speech, don't just be knowledgeable about your topic; write it out, so that the listener will absorb what you want them to understand with ease and lasting impact. How is this achieved? In the same manner as Moses prayed to his Lord:

> *"My Lord! Open out for me my breast,*
> *And ease for me my task,*
> *And untie the knot of my tongue,*
> *That they may understand my speech..."*
> Holy Qur'an (20:26-29)

The Simplest Method of Crafting Your Speech

A well-known format is to start your speech with an interesting fact, statistic or story that relates to your topic. You want to start your speech off with a bang! As Winston Churchill said:

> *"If you have an important point to make, don't try to be subtle or clever. Use a pile driver. Hit the point once. Then come back and hit it again. Then hit it a third time —a tremendous whack."*

You can end your speech by tying in the opening fact, statistic or story to your concluding points. In between, you should simply inform your audience about your topic and give them more than what they expect. However, before you get into the nitty-gritty of your speech, spend a minute giving them an overview of what you will cover. This way you give your audience a track to run on as they listen to you and synthesize your points. If you don't do this important step, people might get frustrated, because they don't know where you're going and what you're getting at. In other words, paint a bigger picture and then explain the picture.

If your speech is about solutions to the world child hunger problem, first paint the picture of child hunger in various parts of the world alongside details of its prevalence and its impact on both the children and their societies. Now, having done that, you could describe certain solutions that ought to be implemented in point form. Next, you would proceed to discuss each point in descriptive detail. This simple method will bring your audience into your head. Your listener will see your views with extreme clarity, rather than them hearing a parade of ideas to discuss the issue of child hunger. It's that easy: get on with your speech, inform, educate and get your points across. In your conclusion, wrap up by summarizing what you talked about; make your grand finale point and that's it, you're done. You can take a few questions and give yourself a pat on the back.

Adding Pizzazz and Panache to Your Speech

Here are some other points to consider and incorporate in your "speech". Make use of stories. Your audience will probably forget a lot of your facts and figures, but they will not forget your stories. You can use real-life stories or even mythical stories that illustrate your key points. As you write your speech, remember that you should take time to identify two or three parts that you know will be your main "memorable moments". Your audience will remember how they made them feel, not your entire speech. Also, practice writing in general; good writing skills and speaking skills are cousins. Crack a joke or two. The appropriate spots would be in the very beginning to loosen up the audience and get them to like you and somewhere in between to carry them towards your finale. Don't get worried about messing up when you do deliver your points. Let's say you were going to discuss five reasons and you only covered four, don't fret, because they won't know what they missed. This will take the pressure off you trying to be perfect. If you follow the basic outline of introduction; followed by showcasing major themes to be covered; body of speech; recapping your major themes and conclusion, your mission will be accomplished. A few missed points will not be detected and is inconsequential to your mission.

Should You Memorize Your Entire Speech?

This brings up the point of whether to memorize your speech or read off a computer screen. The best approach is to do both. Here is what that could look like. You will always be a better speaker if you really know your topic. If you do know your subject material, you will be in a great position to speak on any aspect of your area of expertise from memory. All you need to do is organize your speech in a logical sequence. If those points are up on a screen in very brief form, say three or five words long, you can glance at them and back at your audience and continue to finish your speech.

How to Look Like a Pro

Now as you look out at your audience, look at them with an attitude that they are your friends. You are giving a talk to a group of friends who need to hear your message. That should take off any self-imposed pressure and "butterflies" (remember the butterflies will fly away in minutes after you start speaking, not before). Look out at the audience and you will usually find a friendly person who is looking at you; make that individual a person whom you will look at throughout your speech. If you find a few such folks across the room, you can look at each of them periodically. This will accomplish two things. You will look like a pro, someone who looks natural and comfortable talking to people and you will avoid the hallmark mistake some speakers make which is not making eye contact with their audience.

Purposeful Practice Makes Good Speakers

So how do you perfect your craft of speaking in public? Here are a few ideas: take a course if you have never tried. Join a speaking club like Toastmasters. Study great speakers on YouTube or TED Talks and emulate a style that you really admire. You should give this goal importance and practice for it like an actor rehearses for the role of his life. Perhaps most importantly, give pre-eminence to the job of speaking; spend time writing your speech, lots of time; practice in your mind's eye, lots of time; practice verbally delivering your speech, lots of time. As Mark Twain quipped:

> *"It usually takes me more than three weeks to prepare a good impromptu speech."*

You can practice in front of the mirror or in front of your own video device. Above all, practice in front of a friend, family member or colleague who can give you feedback. Are you talking with colour and flair or is your tone flat? Are you speaking too fast or too slow? Are you fidgeting with your hands or a pen? Are you shuffling your feet? Are you moving across the stage like a cat on a hot stove? How is your enunciation and elocution? Are you speaking over everyone's head by using industry jargon? Are your sentences to the point? Have you used the power of a pause in your speech to add effect to a major point you want your audience to absorb? This feedback will be invaluable. Daunting? Yes. Worth it? You bet! No one said being a public speaker is super-easy, but with preparation and practice and some perspiration you will make it *look* easy. As the famous business philosopher, Jim Rohn reminded us:

> *"Take advantage of every opportunity to practice your communication skills so that when important occasions arise, you will have the gift, the style, the sharpness, the clarity, and the emotions to affect other people."*

Another tip is to visit the room where you will be speaking, before you deliver your speech. This will bring you a sense of ease and relaxation because as you stand there, you can imagine you are giving your speech. Practice a few lines. Project your voice. See in your mind's eye that you are giving a fine speech; see people nodding with approval and cheering you on. Just like an NBA basketball player about to shoot from the free throw line seeing the shot going into the basket before he released it from his hands, imagine yourself delivering a speech with ease and confidence. As a public speaker extraordinaire, get yourself to the point where, if you were asked to speak and were given less than one hour's notice, you could do it.

You Must Believe You Are a Good Speaker

If you aspire to be a public speaker, you must see yourself as one. Beyond having this mindset, you should look for opportunities to talk in front of people whenever you can. It could be in a formal presentation to your peers, a conference speech, a talk to a high school class on career day, a short address at your house of worship, as an emcee at a wedding or family celebration, at your staff meeting or even in front of a few peers in the lunch room. These efforts will give you the self-belief that you are a speaker and a great communicator. Our ability to communicate is perhaps the greatest gift of all. We must practice better communication to have a better life for ourselves and also to help others through sharing knowledge and wisdom. You are someone who stands amongst the company of a few who dared to do the thing that scares most people!

Action items:

1. Write down three benefits of becoming a public speaker as it pertains to your life, career, income and level of personal influence.
2. Watch famous speakers online so as to identify their "style" and techniques that you may like to emulate.
3. Practice communicating ideas verbally and in writing. Use simple language and shorter sentences that most accurately convey the meaning of what you want to say or have understood.
4. Practice active listening and rephrase what you heard to the sender to make sure you understood correctly.
5. Attend a Toastmasters group near you to observe some meetings as a guest. Consider joining if you find it interesting. Or, sign up for a public speaking seminar if you can.
6. Set a goal to give a speech in the next three months. Seek out an opportunity at work, school, or at your house of worship.
7. Read a famous speech like the "I Have a Dream" by Reverend Martin Luther King, Jr. Study it and make some notes. Then watch it online. Be prepared to be enraptured.

Chapter 11
Pursuit of Happiness

"To conquer one's self is a greater feat than to conquer a thousand men in battle."
Siddhartha Gautama Buddha

"If you want happiness for an hour, take a nap. If you want happiness for a day, go fishing. If you want happiness for a year, inherit a fortune. If you want happiness for a lifetime, help somebody."
Chinese proverb

"With faith, discipline and selfless devotion to duty, there is nothing worthwhile that you cannot achieve."
Muhammad Ali Jinnah

Throughout this book, we have touched on the topic of happiness. In this chapter, we will try to give a balanced view of how to experience life in a state of happiness, based on the fact that life is not just happening; rather, we are experiencing it in our own empowering or disempowering ways. One person sees the rain on her parade day as a curse meanwhile, in the same town, another sees it as a blessing for the garden she is growing and looks forward to seeing the beauty of colour to follow soon!

We all have some concept of what happiness is, but how can you define happiness? The Merriam Webster dictionary defines it as:

a. a state of well-being and contentment; joy
b. a pleasurable or satisfying experience

Using these definitions and your own life experiences, you can see that happiness is not a fixed place or destination but rather an emotion or experience that is positive and uplifting. We do not 'reach' a place called happiness as much as we experience a state of being that can be called contentment, joy, and inner peace—all synonyms for happiness. Too often we are expecting instant gratification with no effort. There is an expectation that everything should exist for our immediate entertainment and happiness. Unfortunately, many people try to capture a moment of happiness by indulging in mind- altering substances, be they alcohol, illegal drugs or even junk food. These attempts might give momentary happiness but never lasting happiness. It is lasting happiness that is of most interest to people. Life should be enjoyed rather than endured.

While there are many books and blogs on happiness, it is best to review your own state of happiness in life and create your personal path to happiness and inner peace. Interestingly, pursuing happiness means it is always ahead of us or just beyond reach. To be happy, we probably need to admit that we need to be happy with what we have and not chase it.

Islamic Scripture informs us that God is the ultimate source of inner peace and happiness, as we read in the following:

> *"He is Allah, and there is no God beside Him, the Sovereign, the Holy One, the Source of Peace, the Bestower of Security, the Protector, the Mighty, the Subduer, the Exalted. Holy is Allah far above that which they associate with Him."*
> Holy Qur'an (59:24)

We also find:

> *"Delight yourself in the Lord, and he will give you the desires of your heart."*

Psalms 37:4

Perhaps in all this pursuit of happiness, we ought to give some thought to the essence of these quoted instructions. Receiving the desires of your heart and peace sounds like a good definition of happiness, does it not?

The Purpose of Pain

We cannot appreciate daylight without the darkness of night. We cannot appreciate delicious food until we have experienced hunger. As we do not live in an utopian world, we should not expect life to be as such. Saying that you should be happy 100% of your waking moments is not genuine or remotely realistic; understanding that some amount of suffering, pain and sorrow are genuine parts of life is assuring and shows mature thinking. How you interpret and react to the other emotions outside of happiness, such as sadness and challenge, will ultimately determine both your happiness and state of inner peace. Again, elsewhere, we have tried to expand on this.

While we are created for happiness, we actually benefit from a certain amount of pain, challenge, or just plain suffering in life. This is similar to the fact that we need a certain amount of stressors, gravity and darkness to make life varied and interesting. So, what is the purpose of pain and suffering? Could it be to give us the contrast of life's events, so we do one or more of the following things?

- Change course to avoid more negative or repeat experiences (taking charge of our life)

- Express gratitude for what good things we do have in life (awakening to the beauty of life)

- Empathize with those who have less and face

hardship more often than we do (becoming less self-absorbed and helping others in life)

Happiness from Nature

Happiness can also come from taking time to notice things around us. Heaven, happiness and the garden metaphor are often cited in the Holy Qur'an. Experiencing natural beauty such as a walk in the outdoors or even keeping houseplants, can also give you peace and happiness. Anyone who loves greenery, plants and gardening can relate to this. Everyone has noticed a relaxing feeling spread through him whenever he spends time looking at plants, flowers and greenery in general. Spending time in nature is a great source of tranquillity and therefore happiness.

If you can, spend a week away from the city and go camping. While camping, you will connect to the trees; the earth beneath your feet; the views of the lake; the illumined night sky filled with stars. You will feel a sense of relaxation, peace, and of course, happiness. Treasure that feeling, because it will change when you return to the hustle and bustle of the city. The change of environment to the city will mean you will have to make other efforts to recapture that feeling that nature so automatically gives you.

Happiness from Conscious Effort

Despite our best efforts to be happy, when things are not a bed of roses, we have to remember the option to take control of how we interpret events. In fact, if you are generally a tough-minded individual, challenges will be more easily handled by you. Being tough is great, but why not work on yourself to become diamond-hard? What will challenges mean to you then? Take counsel from the following:

> *"One who has control over the mind, is tranquil in heat and cold, in pleasure and pain, in honour and dishonour, and is ever steadfast with the Supreme Self."*
> Bhagavad Gita

Again, using the positive declaration strategy mentioned earlier, you could simply say: "I am happy; I enjoy life; I am grateful". Be sure to repeat it several times a day.

Be Happy at Any Age

It has been said that people are generally happier once they get into their early fifties; this has been observed because this is the time of life when people have generally raised their families, their careers are established, their debts are finished and their net worth is looking formidable. On reading this, does this give you a sense of relief knowing that you can be happy if you wait some years or does it make you think, why wait at all? Why not resolve to be happy now, right where you are and forever more? Finding the path to happiness is not as difficult as one might imagine. Sometimes going with divine advice is good enough. Why reinvent the wheel? Those seeking good things and true peace will often find it if they adhere to a spiritual path. Unless we know what we are looking for and why, we shouldn't expect to find it. By realizing our goal and seeking that certain path, God makes a promise of His divine guidance to help us on our journey as we read in the following:

"Thereby does Allah guide those who seek His pleasure on the paths of peace, and leads them out of every kind of darkness into light by His will, and guides them to the right path."
Holy Qur'an (5:17)

"Aye! It is in the remembrance of Allah that hearts can find comfort."
Holy Qur'an (13:29)

Why not try the spiritual angle? Regardless of your religious affiliation, millions of people will attest that they found true happiness from submitting to their Creator, rather than from the pursuit of worldly objects. Every faith teaches us to come to the path of their Lord. You will find ministers, pastors, imams, priests, rabbis, pundits and gurus reminding us of this. As with anything, try it on for size and see for yourself if you feel anointed with true peace and happiness.

Money Can't Buy You Happiness

So what about money and its link to happiness? Money cannot necessarily buy happiness, but it certainly can lead to temporary happiness from the material items it can buy. For some people, money enables them to give back to family, society and the world through gifts, food and donations to the less fortunate, hence creating happiness for them. For others, having money to buy things and experience things is itself a source of joy. So having enough money seems to be a requisite to fostering happiness, because a lack of it has a rippling and even crippling effect, if you think about it.

Interestingly though, have you noticed that the happiest people are not the richest, but those with fewer material wants and needs? As one friend remarked, "You need to keep your material desires in check." The same fellow has no debt and a handsome amount of net worth. According to him, one of the rewards of keeping his desires simple is falling asleep within five minutes of putting his head on his pillow. Many happy people are among those with average means or even less. They give their families and community the blessing of their money and their time and also have time for themselves to reflect and be in the moment throughout life. When money is used as a tool to make one's life free of financial pressure and as a way to give to others, it does become a real way to 'buy' happiness or peace.

Of course, a lack of enough basic financial resources can be a cause of sadness and stress which can lower the feeling of inner peace and happiness. In the field of economics there is the concept of "marginal utility". In a nutshell, this concept describes how having extra or excessive quantities of something such as money does not create additional gain. Often, people who pursue money will find that at a certain point, their bank balance might be impressive, but having any more would not really change how they live their life. Just because someone has tons of money or income does not mean they will sleep in beds made of gold or drive cars that cost as much as a house. Their financial security may give them a lot, but it is not a guarantee of inner peace or happiness. So, how much is enough? While it has been said that incomes in the range of 50k to 100k are ideal for happiness, who is really to say? If you use money as a tool rather than a scorecard, you should in theory have the right balance between financial security and inner security.

Consider also, the other major contributor to your net worth (assets minus liabilities) that is, your major debts! How much happier would you feel if they were paid off? Being debt-free and mortgage-free is something to aggressively work towards and will give you a position of strength. That strength would be a great source of happiness in your life, which in turn could provide a lasting inner peace for you and therefore, your family. Over time, you can achieve these things with astute planning and without winning the lottery or being a high-income earner. You will have to examine your priorities between spending, saving and investing and then diligently stick to your plan. Proper management of our financial affairs is no doubt important. The more solid your financial position is, the easier it is to live worry-free and happy, pursue worthwhile goals, enjoy your marriage and even enjoy robust health. Whatever your philosophy about money, it might be a part of the happiness equation, but not the whole of it.

The World within You

After recognizing how little money it can take to be happy, we must consider our mental state of mind. This is a great quote that reminds us that happiness starts in our head.

> *"Most people are about as happy as they make up their minds to be."*
> Abraham Lincoln

Everyone lives in the same world but their attitudes, actions and words express their own unique view of the world for us to decode. Happier people tend to have a different vocabulary and even style. They often get rid of words like impossible, irritated, upset, hurt, anger, hate, despair, depressed, lonely, fear and can't; instead, they use words such as possible, greatness, grateful, courageous, fearless, upbeat, positive, limitless, opportunity, challenge, abundance and can, among many others. They are conscious of the power that words have over them and only talk to themselves and others using empowering words let alone thoughts. These people show compassion to others and most of all to themselves. They don't get down on themselves by ruminating over things people do or say to them. They practice CBT (Clearly Better Thinking). They control their mind.

Often, they will avoid people, news and even media that try to pull them towards sadness. A great tip for many of us is to never watch news just before going to sleep. In this era, that would include Internet sources of news, too. What will you hear about on the news other than war, accidents, disease, and other disturbing events? This is not a way to fall asleep. Many people wake in the morning feeling upset and wonder why. Keep your mind guarded from such things. You can acknowledge world events, but you don't have to do it just before you fall asleep.

Design Your Own Happiness

So what kinds of things lead to a life of happiness? The following quote provides a great summary on this topic:

"Happiness is when what you think, what you say, and what you do are in harmony."
Mahatma Gandhi

There is a limitless variety of things you can do to create more happiness in your life. Just be open to ideas and try some things. For example, you can feel better about the world when you smile at strangers and familiar people. Try this simple experiment later today or tomorrow: smile at a stranger, notice how they will smile back at you and notice how you will feel in that moment. After that, try walking with a tall posture (head high and shoulders back) and smile, while thinking about something that makes you happy. This upright posture exercise definitely has a positive effect on your mood alongside reminding you of what your values are and to be consistent with them. That alignment is the satisfaction that you are being authentic while you try to be the happiest you can be. Living according to someone else's values or benchmarks for happiness won't give you happiness and certainly won't lead to lasting inner peace. Why not consult your own self and determine what makes you happy?

Another great tip to foster more happiness in this journey called life is to set up things in your schedule that you look forward to. The list is as long as you want. For example: going for coffee with a friend, a date night with your spouse, a round of golf with your high school buddy, a Paleo workout, a relaxing vacation, even attending congregational prayers. Any activity where you can socialize with others will likely boost your happiness; so will occasionally spending some time in solitude. This is also nurturing to your soul and will develop sustained feelings of inner peace and happiness. Design your happiness by thinking about what makes you happy and giving yourself opportunities to experience those thoughts and things by scheduling them into your life. Do some daily, do some once a week—but do them. Don't lose sight of what makes you happy.

Happy Habits

Happiness is derived from the things we do and don't do. A lot of people report that they are happiest when they are helping others. Volunteering brings a "giver's high". As we read in the Rig Veda, one of the Hindu Scriptures:

> *"The person who is always involved in good deeds experiences incessant divine happiness."*

Gratitude is also linked to higher states of happiness. We often think that if ______happens or if I get______, then I will be truly happy. When we finally achieve the______, we often come to realize that we are happy but still feel restless! The feeling of restlessness alongside being happy cannot be considered genuine happiness. Genuine happiness ought to be lasting and not fleeting. You can unlock the door to happiness with the key of gratitude. Gratitude, is a "state of mind" that when practiced, can make a person realize her blessings and in turn her happiness. We are likely happy all along, but need to practice gratitude, so that we can see our happiness. Gratitude is the flashlight in a dark room. Start reflecting on what you are grateful for and watch your happiness levels bubble over!

The everyday choices we make also determine how much happiness we will experience and it can be influenced by the TV we watch, the music we listen to and the company we keep. We need to ask ourselves, do we have happy friends? Do we watch shows about peace and harmony or conflict and crime? What does the music we listen to say about life? Taking a closer look at our own tastes and routines can expand our awareness of how happy we are and uncover clues of its origins. Again, it's not a mystery that people who regularly follow the news are more likely to be stressed than those who hardly ever watch the news. It's also not hard to see why people who watch shows about positive ideas and relationships will see the world differently than those that regularly watch programs about death, destruction, and the negative aspects of human society. We should be discriminating and vigilant when it comes to what we spend our time doing. If we engage in uplifting entertainment, we will feel uplifted. Conversely, when we consume entertainment that is gloomy and upsetting, our happiness and inner peace is affected.

A healthy family relationship, starting with one's spouse, is another great source of peace and happiness. So, we must not forget to give each other peace in our relationships in order to be recipients of peace. Peace in the home is paramount to your personal happiness. If you are at odds with your spouse, you need to fix that. If you are in conflict with your children, you need to fix that too. Nothing is too far gone. Get real about the situation, get help from a confidante and most importantly look at yourself. Maybe you are the difficult one, maybe you need to dial down your expectations of others, and maybe you need to choose your battles. Maybe you need to be more accommodating and forgiving. Maybe you need to be less sensitive or rigid. Believe in your ability to change and improve yourself. You will be creating a mutual exchange of happiness for the benefit of all in your family. If you are not going to help your family, who else will? As the Chinese proverb vividly explains:

"If there is light in the soul,
there will be beauty in the person,
If there is beauty in the person,
there will be harmony in the house,
If there is harmony in the house,
there will be order in the nation,
If there is order in the nation,
there will be peace in the world."

Next, practicing your faith with full awareness and knowledge of God's nearness is a major part of happiness even when things aren't going your way. Being able to submit or surrender to your Creator and turning regularly to Him for guidance and comfort is a way to renew yourself and get back to a state of inner peace in difficult times. Allow yourself to absorb the essence of this beautiful Native American prayer by Chief Yellow Lark:

Oh, Great Spirit
Whose voice I hear in the winds,
And whose breath gives life to all the world,
Hear me, I am small and weak,
I need your strength and wisdom.
Let me walk in beauty and make my eyes
Ever behold the red and purple sunset.
Make my hands respect the things you have made
And my ears sharp to hear your voice.
Make me wise so that I may understand
The things you have taught my people.
Let me learn the lessons you have hidden
In every leaf and rock.
I seek strength, not to be greater than my brother,
But to fight my greatest enemy—myself.
Make me always ready to come to you
With clean hands and straight eyes.
So, when life fades, as the fading sunset,
My spirit may come to you without shame.

Our relationship with God ought to be continuously refreshed and developed throughout our lives, if we want to have the comfort that faith provides. We need to remember God in good times; not just bad times, and constantly seek His company to benefit from His "Open Door" and "Open Arms" policy. In other words, our Creator is sufficient for all our needs. In good times we can thank Him and in tough times we can ask for His help. We can improve our happiness levels and reactions to life's events, if we recognize that we have a Helper who walks by our side and carries us when we need it. The following prophetic tradition beautifully describes God's willingness to approach His servants at any time they seek Him:

"Anas relates that the Messenger of God, peace and blessings of Allah be upon him, said: Allah says: When a servant of Mine advances towards Me a foot, I

advance towards him a yard, and when he advances towards Me a yard, I advance toward him the length of his arms spread out. When he comes to Me walking, I go to him running."

Traditions of the Prophet Muhammad[pbuh] by Bukhari

In the end, we continue to learn about happiness and peace as we travel through life. Being happy can be considered a skill that we can develop despite the various kinds of hardship and sadness in life that may show up. Enjoying inner peace is a state of being that can be cultivated. If we decide on being happy and enjoying inner peace why should it elude us? In this way, we will be striving for higher levels of happiness and inner peace as a goal. In other words, once we attain a certain level of happiness and inner peace, we can look forward to reaching an even higher level from the one just achieved. Our soul's natural inclination is towards happiness and inner peace; we just need to bring it consciously into our lives!

Action Items:

1. Begin writing out a "Happiness Generator List". This list should contain things that mean the most to you and your life. Here is a sample of such a list:

    - Be thankful for my blessings: my family, my health, my job, my friends
    - Eat healthy every day
    - Exercise every day for 30 minutes with at least 10 minutes spent outside
    - Stay in touch with my friends
    - Plan a vacation this year
    - Read from my Holy Scriptures

Expand your list and capture good ideas on it from wherever you find them. Print and frame it.

2. Consider all the unhappy times you faced and why you faced them. Was it your point of view? Was it lingering guilt, regret or forgiveness that you needed to give someone or yourself? Make a list.
3. Consider all the happy times in your life. Was it your point of view? Are you planning to do more of what made you happy? Make a list.
4. Pray with focus during prayer. You have formal prayer at appointed times but unlimited opportunities to raise your hands, say a silent prayer and reach out to God. Ask for the help, guidance, and joy you need every day. You will have to do your part, but also be comforted knowing that God is also listening to your prayer and fully aware of your pain, sorrow and general desire to improve your situation.
5. Study the lives of spiritual and other happy people such as the prophets and saints. How did they keep their positive outlook and cheerful attitude despite the trials and tribulations of life?
6. Make that list of what activities make you happy and start scheduling them into your calendar right now. Could Mondays be go-out-for-coffee day? Could Wednesday be golf-after-work day? Could Friday night be family-board-game night? Could Sunday be breakfast-at-Mom's-house? Is your vacation scheduled whether it's booked or not?
7. Make a list of things that make you upset, sad or simply mad. Hopefully, this is a short list. Look at the list with honesty and ask yourself, is it worth the stress you put <u>yourself</u> and <u>others</u> into?

Remember, you don't die from a snake bite; it's the venom that will kill you. As Bruce Lee suggested, view these things as helium balloons and let them float away from you once and forever!

8. Have an attitude of gratitude so that you succeed at this business of happiness. Put your Top Ten list in your wallet and pull it out when you are reflecting by the campfire or standing in the grocery store line.

Chapter 12
Lifelong Learning

"O my Lord! Increase me in knowledge!"
Holy Quran (20:15)

"What is the end of study? Let me know. Why, that to know, which else we should not know?" Shakespeare, in *Love's Labour's Lost.*

"Living is like tearing through a museum. Not until later do you really start absorbing what you saw, thinking about it, looking it up in a book, and remembering—because you can't take it in all at once."
Audrey Hepburn

Can it be said that a person is ever done learning? Are we not always learning, either from formal education or life in general? The acquisition of knowledge is one thing, but what about gaining wisdom? In a world full of Big Data and Google, can we ever know everything that we could know? As we grow older and wiser, the realization that there is so much to know really sinks in. What if we never stopped learning new things for the rest of our lives—wouldn't that be one incredible life journey! How much could we learn and how much wisdom could we share with people that matter to us in life! The purpose of learning can be viewed as a coin with two sides; one is for our own benefit and the other is to benefit others with the distilled knowledge and wisdom that we can pass on.

Knowledge vs. Wisdom

Consider what we can learn from the journey of life. In a broad sense, we can learn about data, information, knowledge, and wisdom. Data is about facts and is really one-dimensional. Information is having knowledge about facts and, like data, is all around us. Knowledge is understanding the data and information presented to us. Someone with knowledge is called an "educated person". An example would be a meteorologist who knows how to interpret humidity, temperature and air pressure to come up with a weather forecast for the next five days. However good knowledge is, the highest level of learning is wisdom.

What is wisdom? It is the ability to make sense of multiple types of knowledge. Wise people, like the mythical Yoda or the very real prophets and saints, possess a higher understanding of the world and the universe. Wisdom is three-dimensional and beyond simple knowledge of a thing. Truly great people are those who not only have knowledge but also possess wisdom and demonstrate that in their leadership and in their way of living and being. Many years of observation, experience and patience are required to achieve wisdom. Albert Einstein stated very wisely:

"Information is not knowledge."

Transcendental Learning

Learning to achieve wisdom should be the ultimate goal and is at the top floor of the "library of lifelong learning". Formal schooling and higher education can take us only so far. Education gives us the chance to achieve knowledge and, we hope, wisdom too. However, the amazing thing about being alive today is how knowledge is extremely widespread, easily accessible and democratized through technology, the Internet and Google. We have the opportunity to transcend learning offered to us by formal institutions by educating ourselves with content-rich free online courses, podcasts and specialized training programs ranging from Khan Academy to iTunes University and educational videos on YouTube. Being academically intelligent or possessing "school smarts" is important; however, applied knowledge and "street smarts" will foster wisdom.

Seek Knowledge and Acquire Wisdom

Filling our minds with knowledge and wisdom can improve our lives and make us more effective in everything we do. Despite the potential challenge of acquiring knowledge and skills, we must persist. Folks who have a thirst for knowledge and love learning are truly lucky. For them, no stone is left unturned once something captures their fancy. If possible, they will go to the ends of the earth to satisfy their hunger to know. The following Tradition of the Prophet Muhammad[pbuh] can inspire us to integrate all kinds of useful knowledge whenever and wherever we find it:

> *"The word of wisdom is the lost property of a Muslim, so that, wherever he finds it, he should take it, as he is most entitled to it."*
> (Imam Tirmidhi[6])

This sagacious advice is useful for every person who values learning and its benefits. We should understand that of whatever kind and wherever we find wisdom, we should absorb it into ourselves. "*One should pursue learning even if they have to travel long distances or crawl on their knees over snow covered mountains*" is another saying attributed to the Prophet Muhammad[pbuh]. Learning helps us to understand both the outer universe and our inner universe.

[6] One of the six authentic recorders of the Traditions of the Prophet Muhammad[pbuh].

In the Holy Qur'an, we read:

> *"And He it is Who made the sun radiate a brilliant light and the moon reflect a lustre, and ordained for it proper stages, that you might know the count of years and reckoning of time. Allah has not created this system but in accordance with the requirements of truth. He details the signs for a people who possess knowledge."* (10:6)

Throughout this short book, we have taken the liberty to quote passages from the Holy Qur'an. The Holy Qur'an is a book of wisdom; it is not just a book of historical events or doctrine and commandments stating thou shalt pray, fast during Ramadan, go to Mecca for the pilgrimage and shun evil. It is also a book of human psychology, philosophy and scientific explanation. It encourages a thinking human being to look around, think about things wherever they are and truly reflect on the world. We need to be asking good questions all the time such as, How can this be improved? What's really happening? How does this work? What other ways are possible? What are the forces governing this system? The spirit of humankind is indomitable and incites us to investigate, improve and innovate, all products of acquiring knowledge.

TV, Workshops and Apps Work!

So, how do we learn wisdom, you may ask? The following quote by Confucius sums it up nicely:

> *"By three methods we may learn wisdom: First by reflection, which is noblest; second, by imitation, which is easiest; and third by experience, which is the bitterest."*

A less strenuous way compared to reflecting is to watch educational programs on TV. Despite the large quantity of mind-numbing shows, thankfully, there are numerous educational programs about travel, home renovations, food and cooking, nature, animals, sports and inventions. Such shows broaden the mind and at the very least save you from watching 'Reality TV' shows. We all know how "real" those shows actually are! Documentaries about society, history, famous people, the economy or the environment can also open your eyes about a trending issue or little-known topic. These types of shows can expose you to knowledge that someone spent an entire lifetime learning, all in a matter of minutes. The more you know and the more you reflect on how to benefit from it, the greater your life becomes.

Taking courses and attending workshops or seminars is also a smart thing to do. Whatever your profession or vocation, there is a course or workshop from which you can learn more. One great tip is to be the "geek" who makes copious notes. When you are at these seminars, you have an opportunity to be immersed in an "experiential" mode of learning, hence making notes, solidifies your absorption. Referring back to the notes a few weeks or months later will let you relive what you experienced. Often, attending these learning forums reminds you of something you already know or may have forgotten. Being reminded of knowledge and transforming it into applied wisdom can be very profitable. If you can apply even one idea from such experiences, you will end up richer in many ways.

There are also many apps on our various gadgets that can constructively fill the time between playing *Angry Birds*. Some of these can be fun to use, so there's no real excuse left for not picking up some knowledge on our commutes to the office or work. In between the hours of listening to dubstep, we could be educating ourselves about interesting topics from podcasts such as TED Talks, Fareed

Zakaria's *GPS* or Harvard Business IdeaCast. There's so much free and useful information out there that a person cannot remain ignorant unless he truly doesn't want to learn. If you spent one hour a day listening to a lecture on a topic such as the rise of China in the 21st century for example, in a matter of one week, you would gain a masterful level of knowledge on the issue. Depending on your circumstances, you could parlay that knowledge into advantages that others less educated on the subject could only dream of. People who get ahead in life are always in learning mode , followed by applying mode.

Make Learning Your Badge of Honour

We owe it to ourselves to continue pursuing knowledge and wisdom to be all we can be and discover the amazing world around us! Consider what greater purpose there could be other than the highest level of wisdom we can achieve. With your knowledge you could start a business, help a friend with a challenge, improve your productivity at work, improve your health, become a person who takes action on ideas, increase your wealth, help your child, make a new invention, serve humanity and most importantly, have a mindset of being engaged in life because learning keeps us young and alive to the possibilities of each day.

Inspiration is all around us! Explore and consider it your life's purpose to learn something new every month or even every week. Can you improve something by learning more about a problem you are facing? How about creating something with your hands that you didn't think was possible before? It could be as simple as cooking dinner for your family. You could also learn to fly a plane, learn to play a musical instrument or write a book!

People who go deep into a few topics that really interest them accomplish great things. Some examples are Isaac Newton, Thomas Edison, Albert Einstein and Steve Jobs.

All went deep into their fields of self-study and accomplished great things like grand scientific theories, harnessing electricity and the iPhone! They didn't just invent one or two things; they revolutionized society, industry and the world because of the way they thought, which was a result of their continuous learning. This was their contribution to society and their badge of honour! Consider how you can create a revolution within yourself and become a better version of yourself and make a positive impact on the world.

Multi-Disciplinary Learning

Many of the early Muslim and other great scholars of the past have been polymaths. As you may know, being a polymath means they had expertise in many different subjects. With this "multi-knowledge", they could quickly synthesize many concepts, which in turn led to the amazing discoveries and applications that we see today. We too can get outside of our singular field of study or expertise and learn about other related or even unrelated fields. By knowing more than one or two subjects, you can also synthesize, improve, innovate, positively disrupt or change things in your sphere or piece of the world because of your combined knowledge.

Steve Jobs did just that. He famously credited the refined and proportionately spaced text on the Macintosh computers to his fascination with calligraphy. Jobs was also a student of Eastern philosophy, the popular music of his era and of course, electronics. Although Steve Jobs never graduated from college, he did possess knowledge of various things that he was able to synthesize into the various iProducts we enjoy today. Jobs, like many other polymaths, demonstrated how various fields can combine. He explained how Apple integrated multiple disciplines, such as the humanities and science. These conceptual collisions became partly responsible for Apple's various hit products to date. Cross-disciplinary study should be a part of any serious person's regimen.

Learn How to Speak French in 90 Days

A friend of ours planned a trip with his wife to France for their 20th wedding anniversary. So, like any normal fifty-year-old year old guy, he decided to learn to speak French. He bought some CDs to listen to in his car and hired a tutor to speak to him in French once a week for an hour. How did he do after 90 days? *Notre ami peut parler français maintenant* (our friend can speak French now). Learning languages is also a great way to increase your knowledge and wisdom. This skill will open doors to other cultures and new ways of thinking.

There are many dominant languages in the world and knowing just one in addition to your mother tongue will give you advantages over the next person who does not. Isn't it worth spending some time learning a new language so you can have a competitive advantage over someone who knows just one? Ultimately, we should do it for our own sake, but there is a tangible benefit for this kind of knowledge whenever someone is competing for a job or entry to a specialized program. Being able to communicate in someone else's mother tongue creates feelings of trust and camaraderie. Speaking her language and comprehending her ideas and views also gives you insights on how she thinks and views the world. Being able to speak the same language puts you on the same page.

Preserve and Pass On Your Knowledge

Here is an interesting concept to ponder. How many generations of ancestors do you know about? Can you go back in your family tree a hundred years? How about three hundred years? Five hundred years? Imagine the interesting lives they must have lived. Think about all the great life lessons they must have accumulated. Do you know what they are? Do you have a book or set of oral stories that you can go over to learn about the things they might have wanted to pass to their future generations? If you do, that should be considered a great treasure. It is likely that you don't have such a treasure, but your future generations can. Start documenting and preserving your best ideas and pass them on. Who knows how it may be helpful to your great-great-great granddaughter or grandson?

Prosper Through Continuous Learning!

In the final analysis, the highest form of learning is wisdom, so let's consider our lives as a pursuit of wisdom to truly get the most out of life. Wisdom is that great reward that makes sense of the bigger picture and gives the satisfaction of truly understanding something. We can hope to achieve this through a lifelong approach to learning each and every day. Every encounter, every thought, feeling, and action is an opportunity to gain wisdom and become a more interesting person. The constant pursuit of knowledge as a curious human being is what leads to wisdom and a much more fulfilling life. It's never too late to grow into the most awesome version of yourself. Alas,

> *"The best time to plant a tree is 20 years ago. The next best time is right now."*
> Chinese proverb.

As the saying goes: *"Wisdom is the highest form of knowledge and applied wisdom is better still"*.

Action Steps

1. You know how you often feel like a fish out of water in certain situations? Make a commitment to finally learn that skill. Maybe it's hooking up the speakers to your big-screen TV, finally learning to swim, giving a speech, or learning how to drive. Do that at least three times this year.
2. Read some books outside your field of formal education every year and try to relate this information to what you know. For example, if you study IT, business or math, read about cooking, fitness, plants or philosophy. Learn to integrate it into your current area of expertise and come up with something innovative.
3. Look back in your journey to the job, business or hobbies you have today and study what things you had to learn, what experiences you needed to have and people you needed to meet to get to where you are now. Try connecting the dots to see how your learning transformed into wisdom and into the rewards you enjoy today.
4. Consider everything you read, listen to, speak about and take action on achieving expertise in multiple topics rather than limiting yourself to just one subject or field.
5. Watch informative documentaries, like ones about how the universe began, biographies, like those about real life heroes and movies that are considered classics of their era, like *Sholay*.
6. Make a plan to learn one small skill every month such as properly tying a necktie using a full Windsor knot, making the fluffiest scrambled eggs, doing a proper pull-up, reading the top 100 classics of English literature or learning to play chess. Have a bigger plan to gain a new, complex skill at least

every six months like learning a new language, cooking some meals from scratch, or rock climbing.

7. Learning about things is great but doing and acting on what you learned is where the whole thing comes together. If you want to truly apply the things you have been learning while reading this book, there is one thing left to do. Take your time on this and come up with a list of **Five Daily Actions** that you know you should be doing. Keep a copy of this list in your wallet, on your cellphone wallpaper screen, at your desk, on the visor of your car, by your bedside, on your bathroom mirror and on your fridge. By seeing it everywhere and by acting on it, you will see rapid results. The list could be as simple as: (1) Eat real food, (2) Pray, (3) Spend time with my mother, (4) Exercise daily 30 minutes, and (5) Read. These **Five Daily Actions** should be your **Highest Pay-Off Actions** that move you towards your most Awesome Life! Once you have ingrained these Actions, you can consider adding other ones that make sense for you.

Epilogue

"Open your eyes, look within. Are you satisfied with the life you're living?"
Bob Marley

"Life isn't about finding yourself. Life is about creating yourself."
George Bernard Shaw

"If you talk to a man in a language he understands, that goes to his head. If you talk to him in his language, that goes to his heart."
Nelson Mandela

We hope we have succeeded in some small way to have spoken to your heart and we hope you enjoyed this book. Please give us your feedback. Please share your awesome stories with us. We know that we have been a little light on providing inspiring quotes, so here are some more great quotes to summarize the book and motivate you to take action:

"Do you want to know who you are? Don't ask. Act! Action will delineate and define you."
Thomas Jefferson

"Our chief want is someone who will inspire us to be what we know we could be."
Ralph Waldo Emerson

"Formal education will make you a living; self-education will make you a fortune."
Jim Rohn

"Four things for success: work and pray, think and believe."
Norman Vincent Peale

As we depart, we would like to share a poem attributed to Portia Nelson, and given to us by a true friend.

Autobiography in Five Chapters

Chapter I
I walk down the street. There is a deep hole in the sidewalk. I fall in. I am lost. I am helpless. It isn't my fault. It takes forever to find a way out.
Chapter II
I walk down the same street. There is a deep hole in the sidewalk. I pretend I don't see it. I fall in again. I can't believe I am in the same place. But, it isn't my fault. It still takes a long time to get out.
Chapter III
I walk down the same street. There is a deep hole in the sidewalk. I see it is there. I still fall in ... it's a habit ... but my eyes are open. It is my fault. I get out immediately.
Chapter IV
I walk down the same street. There is a deep hole in the sidewalk. I walk around it.
Chapter V
I walk down another street.

The essence of the poem aptly describes the theme of this book and that is to move towards new possibilities, discard old ways and habits, claim personal responsibility, and do it with your eyes consciously wide open! Most of all, the "street of life" that you walk down is your choice. See you at the corner of Personal Journey Avenue and

Awesome Life Boulevard!

In conclusion, your awesome life is waiting for you! Go out there and live it!

Suggested Reading

The Holy Qur'an
The Bible
The Bhagavad Gita
Think and Grow Rich *by Napoleon Hill*
Pivot *by Alan R. Zimmerman*
Meditations *by Marcus Aurelius*
As A Man Thinketh *by James Allan*
Awaken The Giant Within *by Anthony Robbins*
How to Win Friends and Influence People *by Dale Carnegie*
Happier *by Tal Ben-Shahar*
The Seven Habits of Highly Effective People *by Stephen Covey*
Self-Reliance Essay *by Ralph Waldo Emerson*
The Power of Positive Thinking *by Norman Vincent Peale*
The Power of Your Subconscious Mind *by Joseph Murphy*
The Science of Getting Rich *by Wallace D. Wattles*
The Lean Body Promise *by Lee Labrada*
Primal Blueprint *by Mark Sisson*
Eat To Live *by Joel Fuhrman*
The GI Diet *by Rick Gallop*
The Eight Hour Diet *by David Zinczenko*
Wherever You Go There You Are *by Jon Kabat-Zinn*
How to Sell Yourself to Others *by Elmer Wheeler*
The Richest Man in Babylon *by George S. Clason*
Walden: Life In the Woods *by Henry David Thoreau*
Mastery *by Robert Greene*
Four Hour Workweek *by Timothy Ferriss*
Four Hour Chef *by Timothy Ferriss*
Getting Things Done *by David Allen*
Mega Living *by Robin Sharma*
Men are From Mars, Women are From Venus *by John Gray*
Letters From A Stoic *by Seneca*
Bold *by Peter Diamondis and Steven Kotler*
The Obstacle is the Way *by Ryan Holiday*
Astronauts Guide to Life on Earth *by Chris Hadfield*
A Message to Garcia *by Elbert Hubbard*

About the Authors

Ahsan Khan: Ahsan is an affable fellow who loves people and sees the best in them. He strives to be well-liked and is trying to figure out life just like the rest of us. According to his mother, he sometimes talks too much but makes up for that with his boyish charm and good looks. He is a good friend, loving husband, busy father and along with his brother Asif, is a successful Wealth Advisor who works at one of Canada's most respected Wealth Management firms. When he is not working or writing, he can often be found golfing or coasting on his longboard.

Shazad Ahmad: Shazad is the youngest of three siblings and was born at the same time as E-mail, TCP/IP protocol and the early days of the Internet... He loves technology, as you may have guessed. Shazad grew up in the Greater Toronto Area where he still lives today with his amazing wife. Shazad has built his career in the Information and Communications Technology industry for the past 20 plus years. Shazad loves food, constantly learning, travel and reading books about history, philosophy, health and self-improvement. Long time friends, Shazad and Ahsan hope you and your good friends all read this book to spread Awesomeness to everyone you know!

How to Get in Touch with Ahsan and Shazad

Please visit our website: www.awesomelifebook.com to provide feedback, place orders for the book, access additional resources and tools, or to inquire about speaking engagements and corporate seminars.

Why not just bookmark our website?
www.awesomelifebook.com